Edge of Light

Andrew Peters

To all who seek Nature, not as a resource for human exploitation, rather as a ground of being, which comforts whenever the crush is overwhelming and sings whenever beauty is sublime.

Including

Patterns in Entropy

and

Where Light Curves

Come forth into the light of things, let nature be your teacher.
     William Wordsworth

To see a world in a grain of sand and
     heaven in a wild flower
Hold infinity in the palm of your hand
    and eternity in an hour.
     William Blake

Patterns in Entropy

Nature uses only the longest threads to weave her patterns, so that each small piece of her fabric reveals the organization of the entire tapestry.

--- Richard P. Feynman

Table of Contents

Blurred at the Edge

Title	Page
Windmill	1
Silt	2
The Blade Has Moved On	3
Consolation	4
Breath of Life	6
Strawberries	7
Languid	8
Amusement	9
Dust	10
Sorrow	11
Art Institute, Chicago	12
fields	13
Winter Creek	14
Kansas Field at Night	15
Honor	16
Owl	18
At the Beach	19
Along the Watchtower	20

Event Horizon

Title	Page
What is Left	24
Sonnet to Icarus	25
Darkness	26
Bridge	28
Moai	30
Wolves	32
Paradigm of Violence	34
Boats	35
Storm	36
Bison	38
Sonnet to Prometheus	40
Lost Currents	41
Ash Wednesday	42
Staring the Dark Down	44
Ode to Order	46
Dominant Species	48
Crucifix	49
Fugitive	53

Watching Lights Go Out

Title	Page
Shot of a Lifetime	57
Decadence	58
Memorial Stump	59
Memory	60
Winter Walk	62
Ship at Sea	63
The City	64
Questions	66
last whisper	67
Waters of Oblivion	68
Hidden Treasure	70
The Past	72
Rabbit	73
Church	74
Main Street	76
Faded Cloth	77
Experienced	78
Midnight Fire	80

Blurred at the Edge

Beauty surrounds us, but usually we need to be walking in a garden to know it.
                          --- Rumi

Windmill

Was a time cattle would gather
at the galvanized circle,
the only water as far as could be seen.
They would gather pressing together
to drink and mingle slow,
tails waving, and some would lie down
in the everlasting dust chewing cud.
Above them indistinguishable blades
would utter their metallic creak
like a historical footnote.

The unhurried herd never wondered
about the paths curving away
in any direction over rolling fields
and down ravines, never a thought
to where they might go.
They knew the way home.
The house there on the farthest hill
would call them in come evening.
Their bells always sounded
like Sunday morning.

The cattle still low softly when dreams
recall the years from wherever they go.
But the house is vacant.
It no longer calls, and the windmill,
down to two blades, stands silent
over shadows stretched
from one overgrown path
to another, no longer
offering any suggestions.

Silt

Streams from half the continent gather
one by one into this river,
brown with erosion from farms and road-cuts,
heavy with all that has been lost.
Here the river is wide, current hidden
in the deeper bed while the surface
seems placid, whirling small eddies
as if at ease and there is no passage,
no transformation of a planet.

Along edges in the shallows,
soft mud is an easy deception,
but there is no mistaking stagnant pretenses,
the heaviness of endless expectations
glistening along unnatural shores.

Surely perch hide in tangles of brush,
catfish half-buried, wait.
Surely turtles and frogs that slide and leap
into the refuge of thick water know something,
perhaps how life survives the careful sum
of innocent mistakes and careless decadence.
For birds it is all a feast assigned
by territories proclaimed.

Who wouldn't choose cold mountains
where flashing spray can be heard
a mile down the path? Who wouldn't be
a stream so clear it is invisible as sky,
beautiful as wet stones in the smooth rush?
Who wouldn't choose to forever sparkle
in the sun's endless message?
And yet peaks are far away.

Despite the search for the thin, high truth,
only dense river is here, circling ankles,
covering feet with fine, soft silt.

The Blade Has Moved On

The blade has moved on with the roar.
Wide fields are now quiet,
but for the constant wind
sweeping stubbles of dust,
and buzzing insects, there and here,
and occasional calls of ravens,
expectantly watching.

Stalks of sunflowers and thistle
are broken and chopped.
Prairie grasses, bitterweed, goldenrod
are gone completely, now mulch
for the soil. Beauty before
danced in the planets breath
waving flags of color.
Now the walk is easy, civilized.

There is beauty still, laying low.
Black-eyed susans and nightshade
stretch the horizontal possibility.
What was hidden before is now seen:
tiny flowers known only
to pollinators, now appear.
Here and there ant hills, busy with autumn,
harvest along ant pathways.

Waves of heat rise at distance
off the concrete city.
Dry dust of this season
rises to mask the sun
in setting, red through orange.
There is beauty in the waning sky,
though wildness be forever in retreat.
Now the easy path is less clear.

Consolation

Flames start slowly under cover
of the cancerous night,
later raging out of control
burning the bridge between our lands.
They cannot be stopped,
though they burn a lifetime.

The fire casts shadows that flicker
and disappear like memories
through the passage of years.
Dreams of the far land,
green earth, mountain peaks,
singing winds, all are gone.

Losses from this fire
are irreparable, boundaries final
consuming hope like dry leaves
crackling their exclusion.
Thoughts vaporize, paper curling black,
words shrivel and disappear.

Parapets and abutments collapse.
There is no return to places long changed,
no passable route to lands of dreams.
Waves wash the ashen shore,
spraying all the lost faces
with a salty sting.

What happens to the mind
and all those shared moments
beautiful as green sparkles
shifting in the breeze?

With the red-eyes of dawn,
a fresh wind moves in over the water,
over the wreckage of the bridge.
Lines of light shine off edges
of bleached pilings,
off wings of shore birds,

whose cries sound like songs
long forgotten that now mingle
with songs of mourning.
Many of the lost faces
wander away in search
of something to do.

The rest remain along the shore
watching the gathered flock of cranes
wading in the shallows,
waiting to see them take flight.

Breath of Life

Calmly continue eating, drinking, sleeping,
but be aware.

From corners
    just outside,
off granite cliffs,
from whispers of distant pines,
and long sighs of grasses
    yielding in the breeze,
and rivers laughing,
    oceans thundering,
permeating every atom,
be aware.

When adrift through
    dark silence,
        desperate fears,
as the moon through dark clouds,
    light flickers.

Hear words of the wind.
Listen for a great breathing
that shares all breaths
    just outside.

Strawberries

Minds meet like birds in strawberry fields,
sometimes singing, sometimes squawking,
always nervously glancing,
bush to bush, road to road and back.

The conference rarely agrees
on anything but berries,
vine-ripened like willing red hearts.

When the farmer comes, gun-ready,
they fly up, dripping sweet juices
from sharp beaks.

Languid

A leg dangles off a bench,
languid in the summer shade.
Air under arches of trees
is as still as a week day chancel,
dark as a cathedral nave.

Like the chant of a cleric disturbing
sacred presence, rhythmic creaks
suggest endless particulars that form
the fullness of moments,
particles and forces learning
molecular fluency shaped
into oceans, deserts, and granite cliffs.

The billion-year journey repeats
amino words star to star, quark to quark,
moving supernova to gas cloud,
gas cloud to new sun, new worlds,
new ecologies and helixes
forming leaves, wings, and eyes,
dancing and struggling
beyond every small death
to this continuing summation:

a slow afternoon sigh
aware.

Amusement

Past the gate to all the attractions
tramping multitudes sound something
like the clatter off hard-wood floors
at an old church.
Here crowds are bigger,
thousands pausing here and there
before bright lights,
or circled round loud music,
awaiting the thrill of artificial fear,
choosing souvenirs.

A few miles away in pure darkness
the swamp ripples with reptilian grace
just a moment.
A heron stands watch,
staring at the reflection
of the rising moon, not disturbing
the breathless silence
that has reigned for millennia.

Dust

Early morning, sun at a slant,
geese rise up from waters unseen
from roads,
calling calling calling
as if nothing has changed,
moment of hope and clarity waveless
before the mirrored surface turns,
covered with layers of dust.

Nothing about roads, paved or not,
seems wrong, comfort in the crossing,
but it is dust, dust that covers trees
and paints the world brown,
dust that forms one face, then another
becoming the wordless icon.
In dust there is beginning and end,
but it is a lie, in all its brownness
a lie, unintended, but a lie.
Dust in rolling clouds invites belief
claiming power, shapes of dreams.
Dust rising from wheels
off unpaved roads covers leaves
and chokes the green truth until
it cannot breathe, begs understanding.

In the evening, sun at a slant,
wings lift above roads
from feeding through the day
lifting hope into blueness
and geese return as if nothing has changed,
as if dust can be washed from feathers
gliding into the waveless thought,
calling, calling, calling
us home where dust is settled,
and myth in the end is forgotten.

Sorrow

Spring knows not sorrow,
hurries from winter's hardships,
relieves with the light pulling forth
green hope from sadness.

Summer has no time for sorrow,
believes each early jog, each day's
long sweat, each accomplishment
left for the next breathless is enough.

Winter needs not sorrow,
leaves it weak and irrelevant,
blasts even fear to oblivion,
beats drums of survival,
drums of metamorphosis.

Autumn of all knows sorrow,
anticipates winter near,
remembers spring long ago.
Colors deepen come autumn.
Empty branches arthritic clatter
in winds of time. Awareness
sharpens, moments breathe the holy.

Life the sublime ever different,
ever the same, repeats patterns
like precious ripples through a quiet lake
appearing and disappearing.
Life the sublime speaks
words of microcosm,
poetry of macrocosm.

Awareness lives every day as a year,
every year, a millennium,
every moment the comprehension
of sorrow.

Art Institute, Chicago

Along the walls, room to room,
pieces of centuries, grouped together,
speak of expectations.
Someones summaries depict
fleeting memories, hardships
and pleasures, how life was lived.

Those wandering the chambers
mumble reverences to each other,
gesturing their liturgical dances
that leave patterns of thoughts
hanging midair, solemn meditations
seeking resonance.

Observing the observing crowds,
the artist seems far away,
almost irrelevant, dabbing at vision,
engulfed in the aroma of paint,
the cast of light,
evolution of The Times.

At night, museum locked,
these works are trees
crashing in the forest.
Their questions echo down
empty halls in the darkness
and are lost, confused
between archaeology and art.

Day returns with crowds,
come to continue the dialogue,
piecing together what it all might mean,
as if times have changed.

fields

yellow fields flash the narrow moment,
    blind

red follow tight-fisted winds,
    thoughtless

wide mix, purple in hollows,
    red angled and yellow striped,
    frosted white with glaze,
    sing away

silent the empty brown,
    upturned and open,
    simply waits

Winter Creek

What does the moon know,
bursting from Earth's womb eons past
to ride the endless wheeling dark?
What could the moon know
of creatures howling at light reflected,
or what could it know of those
who build concepts of time
and whole civilizations
from its constant revolutions?

What does the moon know of its own drift,
minute variances of wandering
that plays havoc with tides,
and in one tiny shift
might alter centuries of history?
What does the moon know but silence,
no differences among stars,
no passionate urgency,
no length of sleepless nights,
no meaning in measurements,
night etched in black and white
like old photos stored in a dusty attic.

Yet at the edge of an ice-bound creek,
perhaps an answer. The author moon
illumines a bare haiku frozen
in white lines crossing the surface
left for those who worry day to day.
Stretched on the crystal canvas
the artist moon reveals a sublime scene
that shows how passing moments
glitter like stars on patterned ice.
Footsteps crunch the snow but do not disturb
unframed stillness at the timeless edge.

Kansas Field at Night

A step beyond
a field of glowing wheat
spread beyond the fading horizon,
telescopic moments sparkle
in blackness beyond belief.

In the silver reflection
we will soon forget
beyond lengthwise facing
simultaneous billions,
the meaning of it pieces
together the face of God.

Honor
(USS Arizona, Pearl Harbor)

Rusting metal is silent.
Waters of the bay gently wash
the skeletal frames,
kissed by schools of fish.
Oil slicks move in eddies
as if the surface might be art,
but this is not art, not wondering science.

This was war shattering metal and flesh,
bone and glass into unlayered shards
sinking.
Swirling debris deceives:
the costs of war are not equal.
Great weapons are rebuilt,
but not lives forever lost.

Remember lost lives?
Remember meals they craved,
their gentle sadness, tone of laughter,
fire of hope and anger?
All were lost in deep fathoms.
All the unheld children,
unheard songs and unknown thoughts,
all smashed the beach in great waves
smoothing sand and rock
and broken glass alike,
all in that woe birthed time.

Despite well thought plans
and well trained preparations,
came the moment unexpected,
the flash of terror unknowable agony
obliteration of consciousness.

Such disaster cannot be understood,
no way to organize deafening roar
pungency of burning oil and flesh
blinding flashes long desperate screams.

Tidal epitaphs honor life
so long as the horrors of war
go unrepeated.
Build a memorial to honor
moments unlived,
but it will never honor enough.

Owl

In darkness silent wings
carve spaces between limbs
in search of the beating heart,
questions that won't answer
themselves.

In darkness eyes wide as the moon
see algorithmic shapes,
but it is keen ears that hear
the skittering feet of thought,
the wind rush of truth.

Only stillness learns ways past
the grasp of talons.
Only awareness understands
survival beyond the sharp beak.

At the Beach

They line the shore because of waves,
some to see and be seen,
others, for the frivolity of splashing,
or to gather reminders of sun and salt
and the feeling of wet sand swirling over feet.
Some believe the turbulence of their lives
might be pulled away with the undertow;
others, that wading waist deep
they might become themselves
the irrefutable power.

Children splash in the shallows.
Small hands skim the spray
or push up waves from beneath
that make them smile.
When the sun spreads sideways
over waves they pick up shovels and pails
and sandy towels, and go home, leaving questions
unanswered to melt into the tide.

At the edge of the sand a shorebird
tears at some helpless creature.
Waves rush the beach like long curls
of a ceaseless poem pushed up from beneath.
The long path to the sun beckons the mystified
to escape the coming night.

As evening comes answers can be heard
farther off shore where green shallows shift
to deeper blue and longer waves
smooth the horizon.
Gulls searching for significant scraps
often circle there like passing years
oblivious to the movement of tides.
They call one to the other
moving down the coast.

Along the Watchtower
(Tribute to Bob Dylan)

Cold mists obscure the approach,
but no one takes note,
walls assumed firm,
business undeterred.
Rain begins to dampen the facade
blurring edges like words
on well-soaked pages.

This was supposed to be
the wonderland, clicks and pops
of mathematic color and notes.

There is crumbling at the base,
grout eroding to dust.
The thief has given up,
and sits back to wall lost in drink.
The joker paces the ramparts
counting, counting stone by stone
footstep by footstep

breath by breath
anything to keep at bay
the haunting compulsions.
Laughter still rises from below
among masses of the entertained.
Smaller mobs aboil with anger
are unaware the joker is insane.

Who will mourn this passing?
Egypt is but a mystery,
the plains of Sumer, forgotten.
None understand the rubble in Rome,
broken and headless statues in Greece.

The flowers of Akbar have fallen.
The Qin are buried clay.

Pyramids at Tenochtitlan
are silent; Mayan, overgrown.
Inca are long vanished;
galleons of Spain, long sunk.
Great cities are abandoned.
Oblivion stands among great stones.
Who will mourn this passing?

Frames of Rembrandt are undone;
notes of da Vinci, a blur.
Votive wicks are spent:
hands of the priest fold
over empty offerings, hold
tightly to dystopic dreams.
Watchers watch from the bulwarks,

expecting the unpredictable.
Words of the prophets scribbled here
and there on the wall are ignored.
Outside, mists clear over empty fields.
Who will rejoice in this passing?

A great storm gathers in dark clouds
on the horizon, wind stirs trees.
Somewhere a wolf howls,
a wildcat growls,
but no riders come as was foretold.

Event
Horizon

Turning and turning in the widening gyre
The falcon cannot hear the falconer;
Things fall apart; the centre cannot hold;
Mere anarchy is loosed upon the world,
The blood-dimmed tide is loosed, and everywhere
The ceremony of innocence is drowned;
The best lack all conviction, while the worst
Are full of passionate intensity.

--- William Butler Yeats

What Is Left

Dust settles a fine layer
across the empty ballroom,
ritual ash slow in the silent drift.

All the stories with their empty hooks
have gone the way
of dissipated crowds now dispersed.
Surplus words lay
scattered about like pieces of a puzzle
forever lost.

Awards have made their way
to distant walls, celebrants
collapsing into the gravity
of their message.
Clinks of raised glasses
still ring in their ears.
Everything ventured, nothing gained.

Here dust settles a fine layer,
dust of supernovas,
dust of lost civilizations,
dust to dust.
Slanted rays highlight the drifting.

Just outside,
doorway to doorway,
the homeless gather all
the significance left behind.

Sonnet to Icarus

We soar where eagles never imagined,
our silver-winged egos lifted up high
on winds of inspiring songs we've made new
from the dreams of forgotten ancestors,
heat drafts shimmering from civilized brew.
Blinded by the fast approaching sunlight,
we no longer see distant specks of life
receding far below in earth-bound haze,

no longer care about the lost beauty
that once was sure to delight and amaze.
Now we have come to face a fast decent,
like votive melt dripping off altars edge,
pure, white wax slipping from once proud wingtips,
faith in human ways now past its limits.

Darkness

They sit on the dock
stooped over, knotting
and reknotting their nets,
intent on the net
and on all those knots,
catching strands,
bringing them together,
managing the tie with the deftness
of human intelligence.

Here and there they test
the strength of it,
pulling strand by strand
the tautness of webbing,
the surety of cords.
Survival depends on the net,
families, communities,
civilizations in need of fish,
silver hope for the future.

Totally in focus, they cast
their nets into water,
leaving patterns on the surface
as the webbing sinks,
soon drawn up again
full of the precious feast.

Repairs are always required
as weaknesses are exposed.
They sit on the dock

stooped over, knotting
and reknotting their nets,
intent on nets,
not on the vast darkness
of waters passing through.

This is no Kabbalistic dream.
It is all so much larger
than strand by strand knotting
connection after connection,
complexity on complexity,
just so much left out of any dream.

Across the millennia
we build holy places oriented
in the patterns of stars.
At night looking up,
we see Orions belt
and the great shoulders
that must mean something.

This is no Kabbalistic dream
imagining patterns in light
unaware of darkness embedded
into the vastness between stars,
simplicity beyond complexity.

Bridge

Screams have ceased in the night.

Laughter also, gone silent.
The bare pulse of the moon
sharpens edges of waves below.

Shattered glass on the roadside
sparkles in passing headlights
like fallen stars:
darkness swallows them one by one.
Some pieces fall,
but the splash is too distant to hear.

It will happen anyway:
a matter of choice,
unlike the rest on either side
clinging like dead leaves to branches
waiting for the wind;
a matter of choosing every minute,
like glancing-eyed prey,
holding each silver beat of the moon,
each flash of passing lights
as the last.

The moon is a soft pursuer,
the meaning of standing alone:
a beautiful beating on the waves
repeats the same round questions.

A bridge is the reason,
outstretched arms beckoning,
rim of night, edge of the world.

If the road loses its meaning,
only the moon and water below
will know.

Standing here is being between:
flashing lights move closer in a blur;
loneliness calls from the depths below.
The railing is damp and cold.
Traffic moves behind
with the roar of darkness.

Moai

Eighty tons the larger,
some with eyes set seaward, waiting,
most facing inland fires
watching over the living
unable to move,
standing the centuries on platforms
blameless before time.
Above any accusations of faithlessness,
these are the symbols of those
who paint faces with mystery
and dance to the great unknown.

Meanwhile
trees have fallen in the forest unheard
and birds cry as if they know
about extinction.
They cry for naught.
They cry not knowing the hands
around their necks know nothing
of extinction nor cannibalism
                yet.

What would the stones tell them
about deathless permanence,
endless mystery?
What warning from the stones
sounded when the first toppled
headless onto the naked hill?
What do headless souls whisper
to long-bleached bones
scattered in caves?

The time comes when rituals arent enough.
Stones go silent.
Unhindered wind leaves no answers.
Lost and starved the past is felled
ancestor by ancestor.
Fear pursues them lost and starved
deep into dark caves.
Lost and starved, hope drifts
soft as ashes over barren fields.

It is human to seek sacred eggs
to start anew.   It is human
to risk everything to become
for one brief year the totem.
But the sooty tern always knew
the difference bird from man
no matter rituals.

It is human to be the island,
wind singing through hollows.
It is human to be the island
that never sees itself
no matter the size or number
of images carved in stone
eyes blazing.
It is human to be the island
that never sees ships
on the rim of the horizon.

Wolves

Ever wolves circle, silent in snow.
Ever snouts to fear, mist hanging midair.
Harmless tales to calm dark thoughts
mingle pipe and camp fire smoke.
The drifting joins faces in clouds,
becomes answers to questions aflame.
Never mind innocent trees cut.
Never mind innocence of wolves.
Genius makes of archetypes a wall
to keep out fear of the beyond,
to keep in warmth of fires,
to keep in fabrications of truth.

Wind, breath of creation,
makes of the wall a long moan,
at the edges, a howl.
Wolves, silent in snow, listen,
as if howls mingling midair
make one long song.
Genius hears only the echo
of a dream long past and fires
crackling in the night close.

Never wolves see a wall,
but only flickering shadows.
Never mind the drifting snow.

Deep in quiet forests beyond,
owls hear distant crackling flames,
smell drifting smoke. They know
of trees felled and fly
branch to remaining branch,
silent as truth, wary as peace.

Now genius sees no farther than pipestems,
has nothing to fear but fear,
while smoke fills the air everywhere.
Still genius loves even memories of the wall,
believes genius is the call.

Now deep in forest soil roots are dormant.
Now owls on branches more tightly grip,
listening, unblinking, waiting for spring.
Wolves in snow circle in silence,
knowing those gathered near flames
know not whats been done in their name.
Now wolves in silence await the end.

Paradigm of Violence

Not the fifteen millennia question of war,
though it often comes to that
pestilence of the human species
that robs lives and cultures
with casual disregard.

Not anger either
though it often comes from that,
nor even belief,
the harmless obsession with meaning.

Rather dominant will,
the fear that defines it,
greed that sustains it,
solipsism that drives it,
drives the nonsense of it.

Sitting in a forest
observing the ways of life,
balanced exchange of energy,
predator on prey,
and unhurried absorption of sunlight
transformed to flowers
and finally seeds of the future,
and the long decay of stumps
to nurturing earth,

nearby in a tree
a songbird sings its ode to joy
as if flight was a choice.

Boats

These boats, pride of civilizations,
have served well huddled tribes
coursing the long river, here quickened
in shallows fraught with unseeable harm,
there languorous in wide deeps
that lure unconscious, forgetful sleep.

Many have run aground or sank along the way.
Some left great hulks visible at distance.
Most disappeared in the wash forgotten.
These have endured storms of truth,
raging waters, other boats crossing paths.

Below deck glory and struggle are sung at feasts;
stories, told long into nights.
None would have it otherwise
than riding mysteries of the river
on boats they love, crafts they know.
Most on this heroic journey
will say it ends in a vast ocean
full of teeming life, though none
have been and back to surely say.
Hope envisions eternal seas.

Currents concede no idyllic bliss.
Heavy with riches, aged hulls creak.
Seals break and cracks appear.
Oars have splintered, loose in oarlocks.
Rudders grow hard to steer.

Mists rise along the horizon.
All wonder the lifting of ocean fog
as dreamed, or whether clouds rise
from a waterfall chasm just ahead.
Thoughts of changing sails seem foreign.
Few would risk the paths of stars.

Storm

A storm rages in the human mind,
revenge and violence lay waste.
Fear issues a call to arms,
to search for enemies,
vivisection of community.
Fires of hatred burn flowered fields.
Scriptures curl into ash.
Words of priests turn to purifying chants,
melodies that refuse forgetting
jingling like coins on metal.
Minds turn blank, emptiness
visible through sorrowful eyes.

Desolation need not prevail.
The dove released leaves hope in absence.
The way through is not
in untraceable return,
not found in walls of possessions.

The way through leads
through learned moments:
learning brief lives of plankton,
flights of bats in dark caves,
chirps of pika high in mountains,
learning the culture of whales,
cleverness of cuttlefish
and orcas, squirrels and ravens.

The way through involves learning
the difficult language
of predators and prey,
interconnected poetry
of survival, sacred words
smattered by oceans,

learned by birds
from Cretaceous horrors.

Forests ring with such songs,
important in the deep,
watchful silence.
The way through is found
there in ancient scriptures written
in veins of leaves.

Bison

The past rumbles
deep within,
rumbling that stirs the beast.
When it shakes there is no more standing
on the wide plain stretching past the sky.
When it shakes there is only running
with or without the herd,
running the dust into clouds,
head into the wind.

The past rumbles
up the pounding hooves
from bone to sinew
into muscle into heart and brain,
two thousand pounds without fear
heading into the storm,
knowing no storm lasts beyond
running.

It is not the rumbling
of the steel tracks that broke the west,
not the trains full of careless guns
crowded into windows passing through,
firing at will,
never asking forgiveness
of the sacred beasts before leaving
their wasted carcasses steaming
on the wide sun-beaten plains.

It is the rumbling that paws
the hard ground and rolls in the dust.
It is the rumbling of heaving lungs
and thick mane that will not accept

civilized fences, that smashes barns
and heads south.

One day the rumbling broke free
one last time across the Dakotas
and on south trampling Nebraska corn fields,
and on through Kansas wheat fields, leading
finally deep into Oklahoma.

The local paper proclaimed
it was the Last Buffalo Hunt,
this one last time
guns prevailed over wild eyes.

Sonnet to Prometheus

From the mystery of craving for heat
that in flickering, gentle flickering
sends fearful shadows to vap'rous retreat
melting to darkness out the golden ring,
we take our pride in the towering blaze
that in its consuming, all consuming
clears land for farms and cities and highways,
and other great dreams of our presuming.

If they but knew, what creature would refuse
comforts of the hearth, safety felt in ease,
or, seeing earth fill with human fuming,
unceasing trash and waste-clogged waterways,
they see regret in Promethean eyes,
brink of extinction closer day by day.

Lost Currents

At rivers edge eddies circle round
as if in clockwise advance
toward the wideness of seas.

But they self-deceive
and in sure decline
within self inward find
the torpor of lost belief,

the stagnant pool.

Ash Wednesday

The heart of the boiling caldera
hints at new epochs to evolve.
Flashes of lightning burn
hope into creation.

Amidst ashes of the prairie fire
fresh growth sprouts anew.
Further seasons, flowers appear
as sparkling crests on waves of time.

On mountainsides charred
new stems from roots arise
at the base of blackened stumps
pointing to empty skies.

Life knows fire, absolving inferno,
understands layers of ashes.
Life remembers cool rain,
predicts the softness of blinding snow.

Among Sapiens, fire is tamed
as protection from the stealthy wild,
and as power of the kiln, source of cities,
forge to shape the metal mind.

The human soul yearns for the hearth,
oven to nourish the common name,
torch to purge the frightened night,
meditative candle aflame.

But who understands excess,
the violence of arson,
heretic on the pyre,
fire-bombs and napalm rubble?

In the anthro'centric era charred
by human devastation the gyre,
centrifugal will, lays waste the unique,
across the world lays waste to time.

Smoke from ancient rituals
fill the air and drift through city streets.
Incense is waved by weary priests
through empty pews at last.

Perhaps the prophet got it wrong:
compassion is unneeded by the strong;
diversity, just a bitter song.
Perhaps the prophet got it wrong.

Perhaps the prophet got it wrong:
possessions will save the human throng;
the poor on earth just don't belong.
Perhaps the prophet got it wrong.

New yearnings of the lost,
understanding nothing,
gently finger ashes to spread
upon the face of God.

Vaulted forests grow silent,
considering anew the ancient covenant.
Powerful oceans briefly relent,
breathless for a message already sent.

In the distance great storms return.
Lightning is heading for a prairie burn.
Deep within the slumbering earth,
a long, slow rumble, as magma turns.

Staring the Dark Down

In the distance a single howl.
Objective unknown,
breathing stops.
Life races the hour, late.
Howl by howl the pack joins,
nearer now.

One by one lights go out
as they always do
as if the inevitable night
holds no fear.

Darkness deepens.

Yips and barks join the chorus
moving closer
now moving in a rush
through the breathless forest.
Somewhere down the hill
comes an end.

Night turns silent,
predictive howls gone.

Eyes open only on dark shapes,
dark on sleepless dark,
edges with no definition,
all that remains
as questions dissolve
like yellow eyes into the distance.

Heartbeats finally slow.
Maybe sleep, maybe not
in clearing the inevitable truth.

Light returns moment by slow moment,
as always with the careful sun
in rising,
resurrection of color,
search for the lightest blue.

The pack can be seen in a far field,
lounging in groups,
casual in pretenses,
whiling away the morning.
Maybe they know something,
maybe not.

Bird songs bring near
the smell of coffee
and the correlated pleasure
cherished in aching joints.

Ode to Order

This sun will soon come to set,
the dream of it, sated.
Clouds now gathering in the west may cast orange
and red like all great myths,
or may slide gray to black, the long,
slow forgetting.

Solipsism that imagined hope
a distant morning ago
did not foresee myopic gloom,
did not foresee that this
was not order from chaos
but the gleaming blade
that sliced aorta and vein,
strands from the net of life.

No matter shining cities,
spires pointing heavenward,
comes night to a world sapped
by all that is human.
Already angled light shines
a blinding glare from polished surfaces
whose meaning fades even now
in the faithless dusk.

This was no heaven for cattle,
no rhinoceros paradise.
The elephant learned performance on command
still led to graveyards that were no myth
of their creation. The polar bear
never dreamed a world without ice.
The long suffering whale could not
envision an ocean too small.
Neither lion nor tiger could comprehend

an end of balanced populations,
death of equilibrium. The sage grouse
on the delicate prairie could see no need
for business plans to manage resources.
But one of all the species dreamed of owning earth,
but one imagined divine right.

Forgiveness haunts the night.
The darkened mirror sends forth images
to banish self-justified myths.
There idolaters unlearn self-deception.
Truth that waited in quiet shade appears
in the expanse of stars. The long sought
enlightened heart beats the rhythm
of light pulsing in billion year anticipation.
A new day is inevitable with
or without the human paradigm.
The very spirit of life itself
will not accept any answer
when there was no question,
accepts every answer, when there is.
Life ever assumes a new sun,
fresh light shining on green leaves,
sparkling off tops of waves,
ever assumes fresh light on branches
heavily laden with hope,
assumes a fresh light splitting clouds,
sweeping the landscape with peace.

Will a fresh light reveal rhino and lion,
bear and puffin? Will a fresh light reveal forests
and prairies with waving grasses
and whistling sage brush?
Will a new sun warm human hearts to passion
for delicate balances and intricate connections?
Will human minds comprehend
lives free of dualism, free of obsession for wealth?

Dominant Species

Perhaps it began with domestication,
cart behind horse, plow behind ox.
You can see it in their eyes,
the incomprehensible mystery.

They gathered deep in mines,
choking on black dust bargaining
shortened lives for a place in civilization.
You can see it in their eyes,
the incomprehensible mystery.

They meet in hot fields gathering crops
that are whisked away to distant cities
offering their part of the bargain.
You can see it in their eyes,
the incomprehensible mystery.

Herded into pens packed tightly acres wide
they simply await the end.
You can see it in their eyes,
the incomprehensible mystery.

They gather in skyscraper cubicles,
staring at flickering screens,
numbers and letters leaping from fingers
through keyboards light speed into wires,
hoping to increase that stock or this.
You can see it in their eyes,
the incomprehensible mystery.

Perhaps after earth has cooled
life will begin again anew,
this time unassuming
that any are intended to be
the dominant species.

Crucifix

Canine howls fill the night.
Oceans resound with whale songs.
Elephant discussions rumble through miles
of earth. Avian choirs make of forests
great amphitheaters of song.
Calls of life pulse in rhythms of time,
pulse in billions of hearts
of every species and living cell,
pulse in the slow birth of stars.

Now life is split asunder,
survival instinct rotting into fear of nature,
justified destruction of the garden
to make way for patterned rows,
pest control and concrete expanse,
pretense that these are eyes of God,
when life sees only one living
in limitless variation,
pretense that these are songs of God,
when life hears disparate tones
in mountain hollows and ocean waves
blending harmonious moments.

Easy deception, belief in answers,
piecing together promises
of wealth to solve loneliness,
power to pacify insecurity,
violence to conquer fears.
Easy deception, innovation of evil,
sweet fruit dripping down centuries,
nectar for those who would be God.
Here is the defining accuser,
birth of revenge and savior hero,

eye of self transfixed
preaching Other as evil,
when it is evil itself that speaks.

Evil has no patience,
makes explosives to manage differences,
economies to quicken the heartbeat of life.
Enters the one who authors
myths and stories to promote
human purpose and intention,
pretense of divine decree,
scriptures of assumptions
that preach only the human paradigm,
that ignore living flesh to offer
dreams to bare-boned skulls
and hope to eyes of terror.

Easy deception, belief
in violence to answer violence,
freedom relinquished, terror unleashed.
Enters the transcendent promise,
awareness of living exchanged
for dreams of unknowable beauty
later always later after
evil has been sated.
Enters ridicule of the thought
that nonviolence is powerful,
everlasting peace, possible.

Enters perversion of the message,
making symbols of martyred hope
into idols to humanity, crucifixes
dangling from necks and hung from walls
now means of profit and power,
rather than strength for the poor,
and pathways to life.

Now the wound from evil widens,
nails in the palms of life stretch,
gash in the side deepens.
Views of interconnected living dim,
within the human paradigm.

Lifes double helix ignores
such fictions and solipsisms,
images that touch the greater plenum
only through the human mind.
It sings the song of survival,
joy of living spontaneous,
diversity reaching every niche,
pulling together communities
of shared energy, sacrificial views
that make of each being
not difference but kinship
and deeper presence.

The call of life seems weak
against sharp edges of sermonized fear,
ludicrous against the crush of violence,
but its word arrives in minds of patience,
like the soft rim of dawn
that imperceptibly becomes bright noon.
Against sharp cliffs it sends whispers
in wind and rain that smooth the hardest stone
into spreading deltas and rolling plains.

Truth ignores anguish,
expects destruction as much as creation,
understands extinction,
regenerates diversity.

If only the human gene can accept
forgiveness, bind wounds for healing,
end selfish ways, build compassionate
community. The call of life arises
from the martyred moment
that will not yield to violence
offering heaven on earth,
understanding freedom in humility,
justice arising from peace,
pleasure that learns from pain,
beauty that arises from desolation
the same as from abundance.

The call of life arises again
and again in messages made flesh,
diverse as the unrelenting poor,
powerful as rays of sunlight,
resilient as community.
Whenever terror and oppression
would crush the living spirit,
the call of life arises again
in words of wilderness prophets,
like the distant call of mothers at dusk
calling humanity home.

Fugitive

Run down the midnight beach,
in and out with the rush of foam,
up and down dark waves
that whisper in rip-tides to those

who know running is as useless
as secrets lost somewhere in the sand
like hard-shelled clams
crawling deeper.

Fall breathless on castles
left slumping with the tide;
roll in the gritty dark,
laughing and crying at once
at nothing special.

At last, quiet and still
except for ocean washing feet,
see, a searchlight gleams over wave crests
from the pearl-faced moon
shining beyond tides.

Watching
Lights
Go
Out

Without enough wilderness America will change. Democracy, with its myriad personalities and increasing sophistication, must be fibered and vitalized by regular contact with outdoor growths – animals, trees, sun warmth and free skies – or it will dwindle and pale.

--- Walt Whitman

Shot of a Lifetime

Playing basketball long into the night,
the ball thuds with weary hearts
in the cold darkness the day the team lost
in overtime finals, if-onlys
ringing in ears.

Pounding the boards,
breaths hanging on half-lit air,
feet crash the concrete court
as if to drum away permanence.

Food doesnt matter slashing darkness
with impossible passes,
and fall-away jumpers zipping
unsuspecting nets
sounding like crowd whispers
in the panting darkness.

Years later, past choices,
only memories for dreams,
clock ticking the final seconds,
hope still lingers for that perfect pass,
the shot of a lifetime.

Decadence

A broken guitar leans
against the front porch,
split strings softly waving,
voice askew.

Something rotten
under the drooping elm
draws the nauseous hum
of a vagrant choir.

Passing jets swallow it all
temporarily.
The door is locked.
Behind pulled shades,

something squeaks.
A television is too loud
advertising the latest.
Belief like a fan too small

stirs nothing of consequence.

Memorial Stump

Tree and earth embracing need no language,
and long after life has left the fallen,
the memorial stump remains embraced.
Each year curling vines
gather through the grove to bloom in silence.

Living, the bond between us went unsaid
and holds us still
through long, starless nights.
But what, what blooms from me?

Memory

The body it can be told
will become the softness
of moss.

There in the glen,
all the rings of life
lose their lines to frass
that fades softer and softer
in the hollow core
into the humus of yesterday,
the peat that holds
the forest of sapling roots.

What of the mind
and all those memories
beautiful as the green sparkle
shifting in the gentle breeze,
beautiful as translucent shine
holding, holding the sun
to its covenant?

There beyond the glen,
only the hope of light
unending and ever-reflecting,
only the hope that drifts
like the aroma of pine,
and whispers rustling hymns,

only hope will join
all the points of light
into the eternal memory
embedded in the night.

Winter Walk

Blindness comes easily:
thoughts bent on thoughts
forget feelings they express,
beauty of the perceived.
Emotions bent on emotions
obscure the very awareness they seek,
realization of meaning.
Sensations bent on sensations
react without purpose,
without understanding or satisfaction.

Fire is nothing without fuel,
without air, without flame.
Life can be spent cold and blind,
inert in darkness,
lost as silent potential.

On a crisp winter walk
tensions dissipate in clear air.
The rhythm of footsteps
echo through the dense wood.
By chance encounter,
suddenly invisible smoke
from some distant hearth
is sensed for a moment
on a gentle breeze.

In that moment memories
of evenings near a smiling flame
touch bare branches of trees
silhouetted against blue awareness,
beyond dreams of youth,
of a sunrise yet unborn.

Ship at Sea

Becalmed, adrift,
the ships engines have failed.
The surface of the sea is reflective
despite floating, dead fish.
Many among the passengers
go about as if nothing is wrong,
others wail, or resort to prayer.
The captain has no directives.
Some of the crew talk of sails,
scanning the horizon.
Others argue engine repair.
Radio calls of distress go unheard.

The sky is unforgiving,
clear and without clouds.
Even the sea is hot,
without current.
Nothing stirs from the deeps.

A few try to fit lifeboats, crafting oars.
From scattered rooms music
can be heard, or muffled laughter,
glasses ringing.

The City

Despair fills a city
so large population doesn't matter.
People feel it,
but know not what to do.

The feeling comes like high winds
on a lake pushing up whitecaps,
long crests pushing boats apart
and together swiftly
out of control.

In quiet moments,
like the calm after a storm,
evidence of violence
can be seen on silent faces,
a stifling heat beating them
into lethargy and mindless repetition
lasting long past scattered thoughts
and nervous smiling.

People walk those streets
shuffling feet and shifting eyes,
clutching their lives
tightly, as if life could be private.

They gather in loud places
swaying with the moans
from someone else's lostness,
waiting for someone
to call their name.

Yet despite joy and despair
mixed far below,
despite pleasure and pain

mixed far below,
despite depravity and charity
mixed far below,
from a window high up
the tallest buildings,
the city appears only as inspired
beauty and human hope
for so long as tipping points
of collapse remain unreached.

And from atop a nearby mountain
even in the darkness of night,
the city shimmers with light,
shimmers with thousands of lights,
just as from outside breathable earth,
such a city joins all cities
and all lights of human dwelling
in singing the songs of stars.

Questions

Leaves rustle in the passing
underneath leaving a path
of fading answers.
Still the slithering forward
seeks the underground lair,
or, in time, an unsuspecting prey.

Movements in curves and curling
algorithms coil in quick defense
against those who come near
enough to see glistening scales,
near enough to hear the forked
offering of knowledge,

near enough to hear the forked hiss,
to see eyes fixed in a familiar gaze,
to see a generous potion bead
from sharpened fangs
offering power and possession,
passion and desires satisfied.

In the ambiguous moment
identity hangs in the balance
between no and yes,
between myth and truth
coiled in algorithmic potential,
awaiting the end of thought.

Movements farther into desert heat
curve the promised story onward
toward the darkened end of plot.
Sands rustle in passing over
the open dunes leaving a path
of fading answers.

last whisper

behind the vacant stare
vanishing is complete
screams within scrape

the backs of eyes
like nails down glass panes
implosion of the soul quiet

as a supernova in a distant galaxy
falling into itself only to explode
shattering the mind into the night

where crystal pieces drift
mixing with widening stars
or perhaps only reflected

invitations to come closer
pick up pieces of dreams
gather scattered hopes
listen for the last whisper

Waters of Oblivion

It is dark
and home is far away.
Hearts, calloused to suffering
are empty, minds, silent.
Words echo through city canyons.

Shadows of skyscrapers
spread across the land
like an invitation none can resist.
Even churches are lost in the shade,
stained-glass windows opaque in the gloom.
The pleading of hymns, played rough
and electric grows louder;
clinking of half-full glasses grows louder.
The din of such music is like whitened bones
clattering on asphalt streets.

Huddled behind the dark surface of fear,
people listen for pretenses of meaning
to tell them who they are,
secrets they must keep,
stories they must rewrite
for the good of human enterprise.

Sometimes people are pressurized vessels
exploding at a mere touch.

But despite echoes off walls freshly painted
and incandescent lights reflected,
despite silent screams in the glance

of lonely eyes,
long shadows turn to night.

Sometimes a haunting comes
not from the past,
but from dreams
not quite complete,

like the vision hanging in a museum:
"Sadak Seeking the Waters
Of Oblivion."

Hidden Treasure

There were birds flying south,
heedless of dark skies, calling
to one another not from sorrow,
but anticipating the edge,
the long arc of the season.

He imagined hundreds of wings cutting clouds,
things about winter, stubble plowed under,
leaves lost from bare boned trees,
darkened skies that mean snow.

Leaning more heavily on the shovel,
he imagined things portentous,
but returned to sorrow,
and found a smile.
How small the symbol compared
with what is, small the gesture
to every ending, the inevitable gap.

Throat thick, eyes aching,
his foot nudged the box of treasures,
and he began again to shovel,
feeling stupid.

The wind shuddered harder,
blowing birds faster
screaming encouragement
over the roar.

The sound of the shovel
cutting the earth became
a harsh scrape. Dirt struck
the box like a distant drum
as it disappeared.

He wondered about wordless messages
and thoughts lost like forgotten secrets,
wondered things about loneliness.

In the distance across the empty field,
a dim light denied the crease of night.
Shovel over shoulder, he walked back,
imagining things about changing seasons,
and returning birds.

He walked through the first drops of rain,
and later, during that long night,
carefully drew a map.

The Past

The past is a lifeless stump
without bristling leaves whispering replies
in rooted sighs to the wandering,
without black branches reaching for the sky.

Gathered, flower-faced in the forest,
we stand around the old stump softly staring,
led by weather-worn wood back
to dreams of leaves and black branches
holding the pale moon.

That stump is but a moment, so why stare,
wondering that symbols dissolve,
dust scattered in the wind?

Rabbit

Camouflaged on the forest floor,
motionless but for the twitch
of a black nose, quick feet
ready to leap, long ears straight to hear
everything possible, warm fur
warm through deepest winter,
warm through coldest dark,
the gentle heart awaits
the turning day, the new season.

Claws may hunt this energy,
human weapons to find the heart,
but prolific in living, this life is enough.
Silent as patience, quick as belief,
these are the dark eyes worth seeking,
the running that inspires,
the great leap that will see you through.

Church

Dust covers the leaves of the windbreaks
in late summer along the rutted road.
Winters its more impassible
as the plow has more important works.

Fields around the clapboard church
still bloom in wild arrays come spring,
and autumn leaves drift to piles
in the yard and cover the car park

where weeds and grass expand the cracks.
The old paint on the clapboards curls,
whiteness lost, and steeple bells are still.
Pull-ropes long ago rotted and broke.

People who sought their God here each week
are gone now, some laid to rest just outside
in the overgrown cemetery, stones hidden
or overturned, words blurred, fence wrecked.

The others have moved to cities and seek
their God amongst modern comforts,
repeating their myths, raising funds
in air conditioned buildings of brick.

Here in the clapboard church, floors of oak
no longer clatter from hard-soled shoes.
An old piano, strings loose, is silent.
No fidgets cause the pews to creak.

Here each year loses the human touch.
Someday the bell will fall to ground
and weathered wood turn to pulp.
But presence never left, always awake.

Wildness grows in the clapboard church.
Last year a fox denned in the crying room.
Under the floor something stirs small sounds.
Quiet wings swish and bump in the attic.

Religion has followed the hectic,
but here through filtered light, stained glass shards
cast rainbows across the empty altar.
This dust, adrift, is the resurrected.

Main Street

Main street is quiet.
Survivors need say nothing.
Storefront panes stare onto the street
no one planned as if seeing
reflections of the past.

Cobbled streets, built to last,
have lasted beyond the traffic
that moved on, speeding now
on other streets busy with lights.
The only light here dangles
inoperative on its loose wire
stopping nothing.

Even big green harvesters roll past
reflections in the windows.
Their loud importance, unslowed,
interrupts hollow wind sounds
at the corners, but just
for the moment.

Fliers still hang on some doors,
here and there historic reminders
of events long ago, signs
of community that now remind
no one.

It wasn't supposed to end this way,
choiceless dreams abandoned
to distant hopes of profit
in some crowded high-rise.
It wasn't supposed to end at all,
lights unlit though darkness comes,
no one to welcome home.

Faded Cloth

Gentle hold of faded cloth
in tired fingers loses nothing
but being a maelstrom
of memories circling
draws all of time,
all of life worn,
down to this moment,

ache of heart,
full to breaking
of all that was,

ache of heart,
unable to fill
the hollow present,

ache of heart
that loves the life
inestimable, inevitable,
slipping through fingers,
crumpled, to the floor.

Experienced

From opposite coasts winds bring fresh
dreams of passages, edges that lead.
We all see the meteor
that leads the tail aflame.

West

Truth finds its music,
germinates the unburstable heart,
flowers from the open mind.
Fingers find creations beat,
electric strings irrepressibly
vibrant, improv of Hendrix.

Chords enough bend the wave of a generation
in search of life that would never be the same
again, life that peels the surface raw
thinking truth might flow voltaic,
love like the fragrance of flowers,
peace like smoke adrift in crowded rooms.

They could not have understood
all the genius resonating
in hot, electric strings
no frame could hold fast,
until felt in a burst of flame
and splintered wood.

East

Truth finds its image,
germinates the unquenchable mind,
flowers from the desperate heart.
Fingers find creation's colors,
shapes and words of irrepressible
art, improv of Basquiat.

Colors enough bend a generation
in search of life that would never be the same
again, life that peels the surface raw
thinking truth could be thought out loud,
love transcend the dichotomous,
beauty could redeem walls.

No ears could grasp
the midnight screams,
no eyes could grasp
the agony of soul
that holds tragedy and ecstasy
together
frame by frame,
measure by measure.

Center

Enlightened edges, reason
overpowering tradition, inspire
joy expressed from freedom,
hope expressed from despair,
identity expressed from oblivion.

We all want more time.
We all would overdose on living
the unexampled lifetime,
whether twenty-seven years
or ninety-seven years,
never enough, always enough
of the soul revealed.

We all wonder
about the inevitable ending,
the final chord, the empty stage,
the silent museum.

Midnight Fire

Flickering memories drift like smoke
from flames shrinking quietly away.
Shadows that danced are swallowed
by the greater darkness reaching in.

Dreams die in the midnight fire.
Their heat dissipates unsaved.
Hands shielding the first spark
from vagrant winds are gone.

Sleepless, the crosslegged dawn
searches remaining embers
for any that might be rekindled
when next the dark returns
bringing the choiceless cold.

The door closes,
how doesn't matter,
even if winds blew it shut.
Slammed or pushed to softly,
deserved or undeserved,
it is all the same,
standing in the yard
watching lights go out.

Where Light Curves

We are slowed down sound and light waves, a walking bundle of frequencies tuned into the cosmos. We are souls dressed up in sacred biochemical garments and our bodies are the instruments through which our souls play their music.
　　　　　　　　　　　--- Albert Einstein

Table of Contents

Arc of Luminescence

Title	Page
Blood Moon	87
Humming	88
Sonnet to Rocks	89
Consciousness One/Two	90
Dancing	92
Opening Day	94
Common Weave	96
Dr. King in Chicago	98
Wildflowers	99
Roadless Travelers	100
Championship	101
Lifetime	102
Mergansers	103
Inevitable Edge	104
Cemetery	106
Sacred	107
Gleams	108
Fireflies	109

Dreamless Path

Title	Page
Hope	113
Cloud of Unknowing	114
Wapiti	115
Cancer Walk	118
Nativity	119
Gethsemane	122
Riding the Train	124
Voiceless No More	125
Relativity	126
Silence of Bristlecones	128
Message	130
Dreamless	135
Third Persons	138
Outskirts of Heaven	139
Effervescence	143
Resurrection	144
Fire	148
Wildness	151

Widening Between Stars

Title	Page
Colors of Dawn	155
Comfort of the Stars	156
Awareness of Trees	157
Basket	158
Parallax	160
Barnacled Heart	162
Sonnet to Wind	164
Ray of Light	165
Wren Song	166
Ode to the Dog	168
Wisdom	170
Stream	171
Oak Trees	172
Light of Day	173
Mesa	174
Ferlinghetti Aware	176
Listen	179
Mark the Year	182
Paradise	183

Arc
of
Luminescence

There is a crack in everything.
That's how the light gets in.
                      --- Leonard Cohen

Blood Moon

Do not be angry with the mystery
peeled from the choiceless moon.
If fullness were the issue,
then perhaps what it ever meant
to be the moon was misunderstood.

Ages of lunacy and glorious myths,
even the longing hopes
never really mattered.
Now with the "giant leap"
there is the touch that disillusions,
that only allows experience
and unrehearsed beauty.

Nothing will ever be the same.

Though orbits continue long
into blind darkness,
though reflections appear
with equal regularity,
the old longing
for one more glorious dream,
one more grand imagining,
one more moment defined,
all are lost to myth's eclipse,

all human fabrication
made pale by the beauty
of what is.

Humming

The tiny heart races beating wings,
fast as light flashing
purple and green off feathers
faster than sight.

In mid-air blur life seeks
holy nectar at the heart
of unfurled days.
Unrested beating rides waves
of time like a tilted sail
balanced between calms.

Then just for a moment wiry feet
grip a branch, tiny wings still,
a breathless pause.

Sonnet to Rocks

At first glance some show flashes of beauty,
pleasing symmetries, angled casts of light.
Some lying about are just plain dirty,
in need of more care and some inner sight
of what might be a possibility.
But of course, there is more, much more to all
the angles, patterns, colors that appear
in a closer look and a wash to clear

what is from what is not on the surface
of what might be a possibility.
Then comes reflections off crystal faces,
the play of light that speaks not of places,
but history, immense passage of time,
uncountable moments now in this eye.

Consciousness One

In vastness of sublime presence,
dimly within the gray mass
of invisible particulates,
lightning leaps synaptic gaps:
order from chaos knitting
sensation to memory,
energy to perceived quantum,
making of turmoil, patterns.

Neurons numerous as galaxies
map the questing spirit,
stringing bits of curiosity
into patterns of identity,
moments connecting arrows of time,
symmetries collected
into brushstrokes on canvas,
melodies vibrant in ears,
or words strung into sentences
like diamonds sparkling.

Deep in diverse pathways
of genetic curls, the throbbing roar
becomes voices of children
announcing the future,
evolution of survivors.

Fear is the curse.
Knowing is not.
One morning a shaft of light
appears through a window.

Consciousness Two

On the horizon dark specks
moving as one great cloud
swaying back and forth
bending and curving
finally settle across the field,
devouring who knows what.

Silent wings haunt the night,
haunt diminishing senses,
all too soon catching
the last moment, the exchange
future snatches from past.

Do not fear consciousness
written in disappearing ink.
Meaning persists past
the gathering mists,
though not as ever imagined.

Some day deep in the recesses
a lantern will be lifted
to light the discovery
and those who see the glyphs
will utter under breath
"God, what minds!"

Dancing

Dancing around the fire, light flicks
shadows from the corners of faces
turned together for warmth
and the magic of flames.
The future calls and they dance
to touch the source of life.
Power dressed in colorful costumes
brandishes hatred and love at once,
reflects from faces like polished steel
aglow in the circle of light.
They feel survival in the rhythms,
relief from the pursuit of dust.
Fear chases their circles.

Who has heard music and not felt dance?
It echoes through mountains and forests,
across high plains and oceans,
and up clouded skies.
Centuries pass, instruments evolve,
music finds new melodies,
deep harmonies, but the feet,
now fast, now slow, slapping concrete,
crunching hay-strewn planks,
shuffling clouds of dust into the night,
still move with the fearless rhythm
that knows no time.

Dance is not the simple solution
to the unresolvables that bounce
and dip and spin in flickering light

like bright colors woven
through generations of cloth.

Time pulls the weary night
toward the return of daily rituals.
It is there in their faces:
the glow of acceptance
and understanding,
beauty of exhaustion.
They hear final chords
as a new day begins,
knowing more the gift of life.

Opening Day

This could be any workless day
hanging on a breeze
like a thousand coneys with mustard
overwhelming even cigar smoke, drifting.

But this is not any workless day,
because under thousands of billed caps
in layered rows, eyes squint
not from the bright hot sun,
but to better see the arch of the ball,
the moment of the swing.

Muscles tense behind laughter,
tense in shifting legs and nervous hands,
tense behind the thought, the pretense
that it doesn't matter, while deep
the veins carry the pulse,
"it does, it does, it does."

At the plate the bat tries a path
or two or three, then circles
as if casually considering
possible answers.

On the mound the ball rests
just a moment in the glove,
then turns and turns in fingers itching
while focus is spent on questions,
questions in every mind posed,
a nod or two that rejects
until one accepts.

Then the familiar stance,
the ritual that could be dance,
prelude to the decisive moment
when potential turns kinetic,
ball, a blur at once of hope and dread,
bat poised with dread and hope
for the moment, end and beginning,
sum of all moments, result of none,
moment that ends all the held breaths
to become the great exhale,
myriad exclamations
unique and unified, ready
as each semblance of life
to bring knit and purl together
to make of chaos a fine weave,
a fresh repetition that opens
a new season of memories.

Common Weave

If you would know the common weave,
ask those who course the wide, wide seas
by charting patterns in the stars,
patterns in the prevailing winds,
patterns in the deeper currents.

If you would know ways of living,
ask those who follow reindeer herds,
follow subtle changes in snow,
subtle changes in the seasons
subtle joys living with the ice.

If you would know the paths to peace,
ask those who live in deep forests,
who listen to the songs of wings,
breathe the green drift of pine needles,
and understand cold mountain streams.

If you would know reasons for being,
ask those who follow desert paths,
those who know where water is stored,
know where life lives under hot sands,
those who see when the cacti bloom.

If you would see light with darkness,
ask no one, for seeking is yours,
awareness also within you.
The hooks of questions twining time
lock sorrows, joys, pleasures, and pains

into all that is you unique
not to solve a puzzle of life,
but weave your precious memories,
every moment in your holding,
to the common weave of living.

Dr. King in Chicago

The city is dressed in gray
for the holiday, mostly gray,
with millions of comings and goings,
faces tight with tension or blank
from excess looking down at feet
going nowhere.

Memories of Dr. King,
things spoken and done,
float on the air
like scattered wheat.
Hope leans on new generations
to touch what connects
a chord in a song
we almost remember.

Yet the city looks much the same:
gray, mostly gray,
except for dull neons
smeared through wet panes
like red lipstick;
comings and goings, the same,
faces, still tight.

Here and there a door opens
and the jazz of a thought escapes
like steam through cold alleys.
Inside, a few smile
in private conversations,
as if believing the parable
of the mustard seed.

Wildflowers

Wildness covers the yard,
heedless of the mowing blade.
They sway on weedy stems,
face always to the sun,
taking little care to measure
a yard-life's length.

They look up at those passing,
wagging heads back and forth
with the breeze, whispering something
about acceptance.

They know nothing
of distances and motion,
varying perspectives,
conundrums of relativity.

The blade comes, human excuse,
moaning the confusion
of a neatly trimmed yard
when reality is clear,
not thinking about the beauty of wildness
bursting from every grain of color,
celebrating the moment.

Roadless Travelers

Lines divide the highway six lanes wide,
destinations predisposed,
speed and conduct regulated.
Dulled by fumes, minds shake
from the noise of vehicles passing,
haunted by lines and laws
and ghosts of human guilt.
Shadows of destruction
whisper warnings against deviance.
Cars zoom by as if knowing where
the road leads, unafraid of being lost,
following concrete dictates
as if they are the only possibilities.

Just beyond the blur at the side of the road,
fields spread in all directions.
Somewhere tall grasses and dusty fields
surround woods that shelter a place to stop
in quiet stillness to pick stubborn burrs from socks.
Somewhere there are no destinations
for those willing to risk leaving the car
at the roadside, doors open,
nothing more than step by step
measuring the growth of small possibilities
in journeys unblurred at the edges.

The sun spreads magenta across ridges
in the sky, as if polishing a shell
cast up in the evening haze
of some invisible ocean.

Championship

On that field, the narrow side yard,
I couldnt match your play.
Legs half as long as mine,
you were everywhere.

Despite the occasional score,
game after game,
season after season,
I was left with the joy of defeat.

Now a grove of trees growing
in our field is over twenty feet high,
and you live filled with confidence
in another city.

Someday you will play on a field
losing your championship
to someone with legs
half as long as yours.

Knees ache from smiling memories,
numerous as leaves
in the sun shining green.

Lifetime

A single point of light
blazes in the darkness;
photon, crest of a wave,
fleeting surface sparkle;
single flame in vast darkness,
one shine on a leaf,
one ray between forest trees.
Now through thick clouds
it reaches from beyond just a moment
through an open door.

In the space of a trillion trillion mile journey,
time collapses to a smile,
like the gentle touch of a word
on the frightened, troubled heart of a child.

Mergansers

One morning midway on Lake McDonald,
peaks mirrored to one side
there they were, rising before the sun,
mergansers fledging a swim,
chasing along the surface,
climbing for a ride on mom,
dad swimming fast circles.

Frozen winters later surely
some of those chicks have grown
to parent their own,
carrying a brood or two
across other mornings' stillness.

The moment is yet clear,
quiet and cool, green reflections
of trees, chicks riding on the lake
creating small ripples
endless in their roundness.

Inevitable Edge

It seemed a good idea,
fun in the making,
a boat to set upon the stream.

A twig here, a popsickle stick there,
twine and glue to hold it together,
it would not be the great Titanic,
rather more the Santa Maria
out to find a new land,
or Magellan's Vittoria
to discover the whole world.

So set forth upon the water
now and again it returned to bank
and set forth again until
finally it found the current
and out of reach it went,
downstream,

jostled by waves,
tilted by breeze,
downstream to the greater river

and further beyond reach,
drawn to the deeper current
away.

There the precious craft
took all it meant and joined
the river journey to its waterfall,
sailing to the inevitable falls,

sailing toward the inevitable falls
to disappear over the edge
forever.

Cemetery

In the cold time when drifts of doubt
lean against obelisks row on row,
white silence covers the field.
Words from the dead rise up
on granite faces unheeded by those
back at work, deciding on supper,
lost on crowded roads, waiting at lights.
Survivors of disease and disaster
marvel at lessons of appreciation
common here in the cold time,
murmuring among marbled patterns
and roughly hewn edges.

Now an unmarked mound speaks
only for itself, a new scar
reminding the blinding white
that the warm earth grieves
even in the cold time.

In the cold time unwatched beauty
glitters from each flake of snow
in smoothing rough edges.
But there is always beauty
no matter the season,
no matter intention,
no matter the unworn path.
Some warm day passing visitors
will see a fresh stone,
newly polished words.
But seen or unseen, green sprouts
will push through, and ungathered
flowers will spread wherever
the field remains unmown.

Sacred

Stories of miracles, gentle wakening,
did not make holy the message,
but gesture saying "hush, listen."
Flesh and blood did not make holy the message,
flesh being equal in the heart of life
which raises flesh from stones.
Not even resurrection bespeaks the holy,
but signifies the message that never dies,
the hope that lives behind the eyes.
No building nor book makes holy the message
that whispers through vaulted forests and streams,
and thunders among clouds and rolling waves.

The sacred intends no idols,
intends no worship but interwoven
life aware, hands moving in service
to kindness and the great good.
The presence at the heart of life
knows not an end in hell or heaven,
but trusts truth in each resilient cell,
hopes for eyes made fresh.

Seek, then, holy awareness, stillness
in the frantic rush, color in gray prisons,
silence within cacophony,
songs in realms of darkness.
Strive for compassion to move
the creative stroke. Dig deeply
into grief, for it is compost for the holy.
From it precious moments spread blooms
with the fragrance of peace.

Gleams

Somewhere else
someone is making news;
people watch passing fame,
changing of powers.

Here,
now,
it doesn't matter.
Waves lap the side,
an oar dips.

On the surface of the lake
thousands of gleams flash
off ever-moving wave peaks.

Whoever is restless,
whoever has no peace,
whoever prays unceasing,
come here
among gleams of light.
Listen to the waves.

Fireflies

The long, wild day begins
in the faceless rush of the crowd.
The haze does not burn off
until the mid-day sun
becomes the blaze of sameness,
blindness of repetition.

In summation, the afternoon
perfects the mindless chaos,
sweaty habit of loneliness,
light that slips away.

When slanted rays turn red,
thoughts of darkness are welcomed.
When the sky bleeds along the edge,
the heart of darkness
becomes the looming way.

I have stood in evening shadows
waiting for darkness to come.
I have stood in the shade
waiting for darkness to consume.

And I have seen them float the evening breeze,
flashing codes of living,
moving among the trees.
And in the rhythm of their song,
they have brought me home
to the remembered meaning of light.

Dreamless Path

Do not go where the path may lead,
go instead where there is no path and
leave a trail.
   --- Ralph Waldo Emerson

Hope

It feels like the last days of summer,
communal ennui adrift in waves
like heat off pavement in the distance.
If it werent so still as before
tornadic storms maybe thered be bells,
not bells of awakening, call to worship bells,
but bells before the final silence.
Creatures of the world feel it too.
Sad eyes betray thoughts that cannot be false.
Only ants are busy in long lines
seeking the survival moment.

Such heat pervasive melts the will,
dripping, into amorphous pools
like wax around the final flame.

It feels like winter is an unremembered dream;
red leaves of autumn, a fantasy.
It feels like the end of all seasons,
the whole of earth subsumed by cities
breathing human colors gray and neon.
But still high in mountains young elk sing
high calls for mothers and hear replies,
and through tall trees there is ringing
in the paths of hummingbird wings,
as if there will always be flowers.

Cloud of Unknowing

Walk not to arrive.

Look not to see.

Ask, knowing the question
is the only answer.

All that can be known of life
are moments of light
outlining the rim of a cloud.

Therefore rejoice in clouds.

Wapiti

Distant in the chilled Autumn night,
creation screams. Even echoes seem
nervous waiting the next release
from the twelve point bull.
The herd moves among trees,
steam rising from wet backs,
necks unbent, ears alert.
Polished horns tilt sideways,
clatter on branches in passing,
tilt back as the nose tilts up.
Then again a cry pierces the night.

Among groups gathered in wet grass,
the bull urges a move as morning rises.
There is no fear in eyes
intent on future generations,
on matching strength and balance,
antlers hooked to decide.
These rituals are elk myth
perfected through millennia,
myth that moves through mountains
changing elk future season by season
molding necessity to instinct.

One evening walk in sudden pause
elk eyes meet human,
elk uncomprehending human ways,
human uncomprehending elk soul,
all creation breathless
in life beyond language.
Again in gathering gloom creation screams.

Come winter the elk move
along silent paths of survival
in valleys and forests deep with snow,
new futures, new questions, new elk myths
growing in elk wombs,
preparing spring answers
dependent as spotted hides
on dappled shade.
Then past the great melt
they move up mountain pastures
to mineral homelands
they have shared for centuries.

Come winter human stories
seek the insular awareness
of ritualized assumptions.
Far from all that is wild
skylines glimmer brighter than stars
through long winter nights.
Along city pathways survival
struggle is a distant memory;
wind through pines, a forgotten longing.
Sooty snow in concrete rivers
quenches no thirst.
Blinded from metallic shine,
they move to penthouse views
that diminish living myths
in deference to human fictions.

Unsuspected by ritual assumptions,
awareness knows the end of seasons,
the distance growing between elk

and human.   Truth needs no stories.
No human dream will save it.
It breathes in the sudden pause, close.
It lives in the space between eyes.

Somewhere far away
creation screams.

Cancer Walk

Life flashed before your eyes
like loud children running.
Anger came and despair and tears
deeper than breath, but nothing,
not even sorrow like rain
running down a pane,
nothing could diminish that flash.

Through months of gauze hope
never lost that knowing,
because of the flash knowing
time never differs, but vanishes
like morning mists,
because of the flash knowing
what should always be known.

Now walking the stars down
you talk in a wondering head,
wondering whether anyone,
not knowing your life,
might see that flash.
If only it could be known,
there might be no violence,
no wars, no mistrust,
no oppression.
There would only be time for peace,
only time to know beauty.

Nativity

Down from the attic, box opened,
ceramic figures on the mantle,
shepherd, angel, Joseph, Mary,
but for the babe, waiting the day.
Until then, all faces stare
at the empty manger.
Manger to feed the world.
Manger made crib for the newborn word
of hope for the poor,
justice for the oppressed,
healing for the afflicted,
manger made forge for civilizations,
mold for economies.

This was the babe raised among the poor,
witness of oppression and violence.
This was the one who lived for the message,
exemplar of hope,
archetype of peace,
paragon of equality,
whose every breath was compassion,
whose every thought was truth.

Decades of tradition clear nothing.
Centuries of ritual only deepen the paradox,
tighten the net of hypocrisy.

This was the one who decried possessions,
overturned moneychangers, rejected idols.
Now is his story touted as idol by the wealthy,
cause for economy and debt,
cause for amassing possessions.

This was the one who decried exclusion
and exceptionalism, who taught peace,
but lived without fear.
Now is the idol proclaimed by the powerful,
cause for the fear of nations,
cause for global wars.

Now the air is thick from corporate greed.
Pharisees and heretics outnumber the stars.
They love the theater of their myth,
the drama of their doom.
It has made of them the fool.
The Rapture they seek will not save them.
Their hearts grow hollow,
their souls ache for meaning.
To those who show no compassion,
no compassion will be shown.
Their unreachable heaven does not exist.
The kingdom of Christ was not a kingdom,
but a refuge left to us
in communities of hope.
Heaven is not found later
but is ever present moving among us,
binding wounds, listening to sorrows,
celebrating the moment, loving beauty,
comforting the dejected, the wretched,
the starving, the crushed.

Do not believe perverted myths.
Do not accept deceitful creeds.
Do not despair. Be not afraid.
Awake now in the dead of night.

Await the day no more.
Listen, for the message is born again
this day and every day in mangers
throughout the world.
Look to every creature for it appears
in their beauty, breathing.
Work with hands of hope for there
it is made manifest.
If you would hear, listen.
If you would follow, find the narrow path
less travelled where greed is lost
and violence dissipates in the high wind.

Give only gifts of justice,
mercy, and kindness.
See, the one who lived will not return,
for the message never left.

Gethsemane

Not the heroic labors of Hercules,
nor the labor Marx would equalize.
Freedom comes not so easy,
more like giving birth, this,
the sweat turning to blood.
We imagine knees pressed deep
into soil leaving impressions
for all history. We believe
giving away choice,
choice is offered for all.

We believe in the decisive moment,
compassion chosen, answer posed
to questions raised ages before
when death was new.
Surely even death would be easier
than this risk, the chance of garden restored,
life found whole, balance found
in diversity, that freedom might,
in the end, mean something,
or the risk that all is naught.

But what of the human gyre
spun wider and wider,
unlearned centuries passed in sleep,
all the world living memorized lives
following power and greed,

following those who gather in darkness
to plot more wild beasts
slouching towards Bethlehem,
crouching, ready to leap
into their historic moment,

as if that were eternal life.

Riding the Train

They will tell you that you are fine,
test results normal, nothing wrong.
They mean well. It is their profession,
but you will know better.
You will know they speak in relativity,
because your hip will tell you,
tell you to stand and walk around,
and your knees will tell you,
one after the other, to sit down, or to stretch,
and your fingers will tell you
when they are unable to close as before,
unable to open jars unaided,
and your shoulders will tell you,
one today, one tomorrow,
that you are past lifting 50 pound bags.

And there will be pains talking,
little whispers wondering,
is this how a heart attack starts?
could cancer feel like this?
what organ in this area might fail?
am I hearing everything?

In the end the professionals
are always right, of course:
you are normal,
but you know they speak in relativity.

The truth is you are still
on that train looking out the window
at all the beautiful landscape
you have always cherished,
always been so thankful to see,
as it moves by faster and faster
in the increasing blur.

Voiceless No More

For so long their eyes were like flashlights
in the voiceless forest.
For so long they had always heard
everything and vanished upon approach.

Now trees have fallen, there and there,
and the panther has returned
and moves with great stealth through the shade.
So now they, too, raise their voices,
great screeches and howls,
Ginsberg howls,
ringing through the upper canopy,
echoing through barren valleys,

not because suddenly they have found
a new voice, but now they know
to use their voices
before it is too late.

Relativity

Survival depended on knowing
what plants could be eaten
or used as salve or clothes,
knowing where beasts would drink,
behavior of predators and prey,
migrations of herds,
where winding streams went.
Survival depended on explanations,
stories told in gatherings, fire by fire,
night by night remembering
patterns in the sky that knew things
like when the cold would come,
remembering what makes fire spring forth,
and how to melt and hammer and shape
rock into weapons and symbols
of what it means to sit in gatherings
fire by fire, night by night together,
faces warmed within the glow.

Survival depended on weaving
stories and symbols together
to match the weave of chromosomes
into hearts and minds and sinews
of family, those who share
food and pain, wandering and sleep,
memories and sorrows, those who wear
ancestry woven into colorful scarves
and robes, and jewelled raiments,
and who drape comfort for lost years
like strips of cloth around battered feet.
Survival depended on stories
to inspire refuge and dispel fear,
to answer the unanswerable,
to question the unquestionable,

to discover patterns of meaning,
to make of meaning deathless living.

Looking face to face around the fire,
they made of stories a mold for truth
to shape families into gathered tribes,
and tribes into civilizations
that require ever more discovery,
ever more knowing how and why.
Looking face to face around the fire,
they felt hidden from darkness,
the world shaped into their likeness,
and having made of living endless rituals,
felt they had pathways to eternity.

Yet the pursuit of knowing, ceaseless
discovery, led to numbers
and measurements in wandering
without trails into cold and dark,
into sunlight and rain to see
deserts and forests, plains and oceans,
mountains on the moon,
moving shadows on jupiter.
The inexorable search led
to unmolded stories from thinking,
thinking other ways to discover
sources of disease and inherence,
transformations of energy,
time moving in great circles,
light bending around stars,
and the music of the spheres,
the sound of speed collapsing
to both quantum and wave.

Silence of the Bristlecones

The wire is stretched as if for walking,
as if chasms are everywhere.
It is the wire of those hanging from silk,
falling miles, skimming clouds,
holding wind like spiders
seeking the far post.
Salvation hangs in the tension.
Meaning fills the billowing sail
whose self-sewn stitches, like scribbled words,
determine the shape of human lives.

Before the dawn of civilizations
high at the rim of the tree line,
certain trees sprouted a forest
no Pharoah would ever see,
no Viking discover,
nor Empire value for import.
Yet these trees have survived
thousands of high wind seasons,
thousands of droughts,
thousands of snow drifts
higher than tree tops,
thousands of fires.
Some have stood in bristlecone silence
while every human war spent
countless human lives,
while every song and book were written,
every myth imagined, every bell tolled.
They spread roots while great highways
Bound earth in shackles of commerce,

and noisy cities burgeoned,
buildings reaching for the sky.

In bristlecone silence
there are no stitches or wires,
no comforts, no fears.
Singed black with learning
survival through cleansing fires
that burst cones for future generations,
this wood is bleached white with wisdom.
In bristlecone silence
memories are forever green,
belief, a rolling fog lifting from snowy peaks.

It is human to live fleeting seasons,
to burn deciduous thoughts,
but having breathed forest air
deep in millennial shade,
perhaps human living might deserve
bristlecone presence.
Perhaps far across the wide basin
where human wires glisten in darkness
the passion of a single moment
might remember bristlecone silence.

Message

1. Tyrant message

Unknown to the chill wind,
fear hides its viral pestilence
within the folds of her rippling cape.
The innocent night is ignorant
of terror shifting its fungal disguise
along the edges of her silence.
Hidden deep within the calm
dispassion of space,
sorrow spreads its hollow ache
over unimaginably vast stillness.

The tyrant message knows these things,
the hopelessness of insidious oppression.
The tyrant message seizes
their lurking power, promising
futures that need no present,
present that needs no future.

Tyrant message, power of powers,
speaks and religions follow.
Tyrant message, word of fear,
speaks and civilizations advance
one on the other as if
tyrant messages differ.

Tyrant prisms color the world's pathways
shade by shade as if each color
needs no other, as if all shades
lead to black.

2. Truth

Search the rubble
for unexplainable patterns.
Hold here the arm of Zeus,
the eye of Venus,
there, the leg of Ishtar,
ear of Ganesha,
hand of Inanna.
Obelisks are toppled,
glyphs no longer understood,
precious ochers faded.
Masks have shattered.
Feel the broken edges of stone.

Surely it is time. Long since
mountains have grown silent.
Molten archetypes have cooled.
The quetzal will come no more.
Feathered wisdoms are extinct.
Even the stars are mute,
moving now faster and faster away,
no longer offering advice.

The chalice is empty.
Believers once drunk with blood,
now search no more, but dream
backward as if the past
might be carved into stone
again anew.

Surely it is time.
Whatever was redeemed

is redeemed. All is forgiven.
Fear not for truth may yet be found.
Fear not for there may yet be peace.
Fear not for only fearless
will there be compassion.

3. Life

Stretched taut as a blanket on a loom,
the quantum fabric dips
wherever hands of gravity
cup around quivering probabilities,
dips when stars collapse,
dips when stars burst into being
and light is born.
Stretched taut across boundaries
of dimensions, taut on pillars of time,
energy pools on the surface
fusing vibration into time-soaked
presence, weaving radiation into
the perceivable moment.
Light becomes color.
Quarks become atoms,
one moment twined to the next.

This is the story that contains all stories,
the story of colliding galaxies
and billion year drifts of silence.
It is the story of unmeasurable energy,
as well as the story of unknowable microcosm.
No human knows the beginning.
No human knows the ending,

none knows but the slightest breath
of what has been or will be.
It is art that has the ultimate freedom
to create itself.

This is the story of awareness
longing to be shared,
choiceless choice for freedom
at all costs, the long wait
in silence as time moves to effect,
stars begetting stars and galaxies,
planets and moons, fires of fusion
creating the new, shaping amino
sensations, the birth of perspective.
From vast darkness there is light,
from symmetry, asymmetry,
from asymmetry, symmetry.

Truth, the wordless sigh,
needs no exegesis,
no legal fist.
Beauty, the first tone,
twists algorithmic vibrance
into songs of spheres,
rhythmic beat of moments
spiraling into breathing beings.
Love, the inherence
of entangled presence,
learns the manifest touch of time.
Awareness begins with meaning,
word by word sparkling

that shimmers into vast languages
ceaselessly speaking.
Awareness becomes resonant
with the sublime that sees the fires of suns
become the stalk of a single flower
waving in a planetary breeze.
Awareness, the hope of billions,
awakens in humble songs shared
among the migrant poor.

Blessed are minds unloosed from importance
for they partake of the bread of living.
Blessed are eyes unclouded
by hubristic fictions for they see
beauty woven into the tension
of conscious moments smiling.
Blessed are hearts impassioned for truth
for they partake of the wine of heaven.

Dreamless

On a windless night they can be heard,
minds racing, nails clicking,
scraping the darkness.
They become darkness
moving starless through forests and ocean deeps,
moving, moving shapes indiscernible,
threatening what is,
threatening futures.

You can see their vague form
in corners of mirrored eyes rush for the hiding,
waiting for time to be right.
They become thoughts
emerging from emotional compost
as myths of what can never be,
buried solipsism bursting forth
as with stories to replace all stories.

Know them. Know what they are not:
not the dream they pretend,
but darkness wielded
as a blade splitting the world,
and light waved as a torch
to scourge the purity of life.
Destruction spreads in their careless wake.
Many are lost in their debris,
flotsam moments adrift on mirrored glass.

They intend distraction to inspire the running,
running not to the wealth or safety they preach,
but rather running pall mall away.
By day their hoard of darkness

collapses to events
as myths bond to the tangible,
myths to dream the deathless and timeless.
From their narrative emerges perspective, the wall,
sapiens innovation,
layer on layer mounting
generation to generation.

Dream upon dream, formless thoughts
whirl clouds of unknowing into words congealed,
ideas sharpened into spears and knives
scraping hides, edges cutting soil into crops,
painting stories in caves.
Dream upon dream, temples grow
like sunflowers facing the sun,
dreaming deeper myths,
as if the light that inspires could be enough
to quell the fears of night,
as if dreamers could be enough
for all the blind followers.

Myth upon myth civilizations grow,
rubble piled upon rubble
burying the weight of extremes
and horrors of forgotten wars,
each new skyline pulled from the future
by heavy chains of technology,
every language fresh with words
of hope and wealth, promising
eternal meaning unknowable.

The dream of wealth came not
from the heart of God.

The dream of rule came not
from the power of life.
The spiraled core had never
the exceptional thought,
planned only for diverse,
narrow chances of survival.
And so here we are, living the futureless dream,
grasping for death's defeat
rather than holding close
the sublime beauty of living moments.

Here we are one tipping point away
from extinction to end all extinctions,
unless,
unless the dreamless path is found.

Third Persons

Sitting in a room surrounded by themselves
chatting talk turns inevitably among first persons
to their poetry, as if the breathing woods
cared about forms, such crafting of words.

Similarly the flock of sparrows in a flurry
of honeysuckle yammer on
and then they are gone.
Even the minor waterfalls
of the Rockies drown them out.

Mockers high on light poles in cities
have the decency of mimicry,
second person songs that beg an ear
to hear domain proclaimed,
sundering of the world.

Farther out across open fields
or more often deeper in dim forests,
third persons reverberate
a flash of red, specklings of brown.

Those who listen will know
the history of their species,
the future of their soul.

Outskirts of Heaven
Epiphany

Stepping into the bare-boned night,
mortal truths are hard; freedom, fearful.
A foreign sound in the darkness
quickens the heart.
Midnight arrives lonely
waving impossible questions.
In that black sky faces are forgotten;
names, red-shifted abstractions.
Identity dissipates like a breath
on a glass pane, importance,
like smoke in a high wind.

Cold depths of fear absorb belief
leaving the pretense of sleep
in lives of quiet desperation.
Long silence summons the violent fringe:
life, a distant past, becomes
someone elses syringe;
futures that dont exist,
fairy tales in gilt frames.

The path is wide that relinquishes
freedom, follows faithless leaders
who need no answers but rules,
no kinship but the golden idol,
no relation but pleasure,
no meaning but rubrics.
No amount of excess is enough
to fill the faithless heart.

We long for the light,
the word that connects life,
stories to direct time.
We seek what has been foretold,
myths in the stars to explain
the rise and fall of civilizations.
We seek the king above all kings,
power above all powers
to come among us, save us
from injustice, tyranny, hopelessness,
save us from ourselves.

We seek what we have been told
is in the changeless stars,
a sign of justice, message of peace,
the one who cures illness and madness,
calms our fears, lightens our despair.
We seek the star that leads
over rolling hills to a place
where we may anoint our manifest God,
initiate a deathless paradise.

Awake, for stars have written nothing.
Their alignment follows larger designs.
Darkness between them increases.
Awake, for all that built
community and civilization
alike now fade like echoes
down canyons of time.
The place sought long ago
has been abandoned. God manifest
is among refugees seeking
another country far from tyrant fears.

Across the earth a great need
has deepened in the human era.
The path intended toward safety
has entered a wide desert.
The net of life goes unmended,
ends frayed from the weight of commerce.

Do not be afraid for fear is irrelevant.
Worry not, for worry, also, irrelevant.
Tyrant and master use fear as power
but it is irrelevant.

Do not be afraid.
Myths are not gone, but recast.
The dance now staged
requires new rhythms, fresh steps.

Listen, for fear and power
are but one story.
There is another way
older than power,
older than civilization.
Listen to the poor for the message
manifest arises among them
age to age, time after time,
whenever survival is at risk.

Ever present light goes before us.
Yes, light from the beginning of time
can be seen shining from the eyes
of every creature, shining from leaves,
shining even buried in pearled shells,
and jagged rocks. Seek not reflected
light from solipsist pursuits.

Rather lay down frankincense
before those who practice justice;
myrrh before those who practice compassion;
gold before those who truly love
the precious beauty of living.

Live to discern the message of hope
written on faces of the oppressed.
Live to discover the path of peace
laid through the diversity of life.
Traveling that path we might find
messiahs in the millions,
community on the outskirts of heaven.

Effervescence

Bubbles rise at different speeds,
sparkling up glasses
like laughter shared.

Whole worlds rise there
through dreams of life
made viscous by time.

A bottle on a table knows
isolation as an open window:
long wind-sounds over glass rims.

Palms of eyes cup liquid solitude
in sipping foam from the surface
of the mind aware.

Curtains rippling with freedom
repeat the rustlings of grain
in distant fields.

The empty bottle hums
long notes that follow
evening winds through shade.

Resurrection

Unforgettable violence,
the wooden frame for hanging,
nails for building used
as instruments of death
piercing the wholeness of life,
blood of humanity soaking the earth.
On that distant hill sounds
of city commerce are normal,
order prevails.
Nearby agony grows silent
as breathing is lost,
nature split asunder.
The shadow soaked red
stretches over centuries,
over every battlefield,
symbol of power over living,
legislated answer to dissent.

Early morning fog lifts
gently from the land
leaving definitions, perspective.
Vague forms become trees, birds,
a garden of peace.
Squint and fractal patterns
are still there in the web of life
that fills every niche.
Life, the great healer,
resurrects the enduring message:
wholeness is the key,
every species, every being

creating breath by breath
the great breathing,
the biotic summons that draws
life from death.

But though the message repeats
in every vein of every leaf,
that greens, then yellows,
then shrivels to dust,
still axe upon axe insists
upon the human way,
the thought that exclusion
means something,

It is happening again:
unforgettable violence,
oppressed centuries.
Suffering, the great river,
courses the land, now deep,
now wide, now narrow,
now shallow shouting ever-present
threats of pain and death.
Shadows of a cross stretch
over mountains, across oceans,
covering widening deserts, melted snow.
Wheels of great machines
leave wide tracks over the earth,
carcasses cast aside.
Creatures retreat or advance anew
in final desperation.
Pounding nails sound like gunshots.

Everywhere water and air fill
with industrial poisons.
The sounds of city commerce
are normal, but order
does not prevail. Chaos reigns,
nature split asunder.

Why have we forsaken ourselves,
hoarding fleeting pleasures,
thinking the next life we dream
is the one we can cherish?
The destroyer ever is destroyed,
blind to choice, unwilling to accept
the answer to violence,
willing to risk extinction.

But furrows plowed no blade can hold.
In time earth seals for planted crops
to reach the harvest.
And in more time the planted
yield to wildness, the symbiotic way.

Spiraled memory knows extinction,
remembers adaptation,
celebrates resilience.
Its message breaks the sword,
unhinges the cross to make of it compost,
makes of craters deep lakes
abundant with fish.
Its message is an invitation:
be not afraid and learn the weave of life;
be as one and know the beauty
of the butterfly fresh from its chrysalis.

There will be a morning
when mists will lift again
with or without the human view.
Life, the great healer,
will sprout from patient seeds.
The vine will send forth tendrils.
The smallest spiral memory
will spread again the enduring message,
the one that will last
as long as there are stars.

Fire

The world had forgotten the message
gone silent from the tyranny of religions,
conspiracy of hegemonies.
A few remembered stories
lay about like scattered branches
from a broken tree, now fruitless
though the season had come.

Those who sought a new Moses
found them twig by twig,
kindling for a flame
that would change the world.
The ancient message was born again,
passion for servitude,
reverence for life,
the hope of community,
the narrow way that leads to peace.
It sparked a wildfire burning Rome,
burning the heart of civilizations,
consuming mythologies,
names of gods drifting
as smoke over temple ruins.

Some saw in the fire
a sign of power,
made of it a great forge
for armor, and formed it
into hearths to give warmth
for a new civilization.
The fire grew, pilot light
for the exceptional creature,
flame to engulf all flames.

It lit the silk road that led
to stone walls and cathedral spires,
idols of wood and bone.
The love of community
and passion for servitude
became confused with economy of scale
and rights of nations.

The fire grew in industrial boilers,
engines of ingenuity that crushed
everything into the path for energy,
even the warped message itself,
leaving piles of waste to the future.
The enormity of the planet
is too small for its unlimited growth.
It will not always sustain
a dominant species
or unheeded waste of time,
the chemical need for pride.
Arguments of economy,
politics, and religion
are nothing to the bare-boned face
of extinction, the vision
of a planet reduced to microbes.

The world has again forgotten the message
gone silent from the tyranny of religions,
conspiracy of hegemonies.
It is time for the fire to go wild,
to break free from human restraints,
to burn the myths of civilization,
kingdoms of greed and fear,
time to consume borders of nations,

lay waste material obsessions.
Embers have gone unstirred too long.
It is time for sparks of fearless compassion
and the boundless heat of reverence.

It is time to study the holy book of life,
each creature a spoken word,
each plant a living story,
each species a language to comprehend.
It is time to quell the violent fringe,
to choose the grace of equality,
the hope of community,
time to take the interdependent breath.

Listen. Communities are aflame
who would live the day
afresh and unassumed.
It is time for new torches
to light the path home,
to light the way of life.
It is not too late
for green shoots to spring
from charred fields.

Wildness

Wildness beats in the heart of everything.
Questions sometimes catch updrafts on hawk wings,
float in wide circles keen eyes
watching for slightest movements in the grass.
Sometimes they swim beneath
the journeying vessel always keeping up,
eyeing those on board from the surface,
then leaping clear before
disappearing into the depths.

Answers sometimes lie still in thickets,
curled odorless in spotted hides,
motionless until dangers pass.
Or, sometimes they gather in hives,
building honeyed combs to feed
future generations all issuing
from the mysterious, invisible queen.
Wildness beats in the heart of everything.

Compassion wraps powerful wings
around the young, protecting, feeding,
encouraging, until the day comes to fly.
Freedom stirs in the chrysalis,
breaking forth with bright wet wings,
ready to unfurl the colorful migration.
Hope holds close the infant future
in the den, thick fur wrapped warm.
Wildness speaks from the heart of everything.

Greed scurries on quick feet
often in the dark finding any small crack
to plunder the cache of nourishments.
Crowded schools of fear dart place to place
fast as the silver flash of scales,
or sometimes fear coils tightly,
ready to strike with a poisonous defense.
Wildness speaks from the heart of everything.

Justice lifts head to the wind
sniffing for prey, sniffing for hunter.
Patient truth awaits the dawn,
enduring storm after storm.
Feathered wisdom can be seen flying,
flying innumerable returns to give
all it can regurgitate to fledglings.
Wildness beats in the heart of everything.

Resilience rebuilds a web every day,
or twice a day, or ten times a day,
rebuilds the broken dam
across a mountain stream,
gnawing down tree after tree,
saving home and family,
saving the larger ecology.
Wildness believes in re-awakening.

From deepest depths love lifts
the helpless to the surface to breathe,
encourages the next generation
high atop a tree to fly.
Wildness explores every niche,
resounds in every moment with life,
seeks the next unfolding,
the next variant of the vibrant song,
Wildness beating in the heart of God.

Widening Between Stars

So the darkness shall be the light,
And the stillness the dancing.
--- T. S. Eliot

All over the sky a sacred voice is
calling your name.
--- Black Elk

Colors of Dawn

Windshields full of empty crosses
take to the streets in search
of the nearest super mart,
rows of goods stacked for display.

Some stay home enjoying shade
on the front porch drinking drinks,
rocking as always waiting
with lazy spoons for the parade.

Others lounge on corners
talking as if nothing has changed
as if nothing ever changes
unaware when the light turns green.

Most of the rest follow screens
in silence looking for something
that might have life only finding
a path to soulless futures.

One day, one important day,
air filled with dust and ash,
broken and lost suddenly past tipping
find their way back, tired of self:

awareness spreading like colors of dawn
awareness spreading like colors of dawn

Comfort of the Stars

Hours are not enough, slipping through veins,
addiction crying out for more never enough.
Daytime, sun high, moments crowded
with responsibilities struggle
to become possibilities.
Sadness crowds them to the top,
effervescing at last irretrievably.

Nighttime darkness swallows
perspectives, swallows
probabilities, whispers years,
like a mother to her crying child.
Somewhere in the darkness
between the widening stars,
the decades slip away and are lost.

Across vast distances that mock
the thought of time, lifetimes blink,
perspectives reverse, horizons
disappear, loss unimagines.
Small impossibilities whisper
the Hawking solution and blackness
shimmers with harmonies of hymns
that will not be forgotten.

From there, almost invisible,
a blue planet can be seen
where blinks mortal souls,
where spins seasons in well-timed
repetitions, new buds and fresh leaves
uncurled spreading like gold through clouds
deep in the presence of morning light.

Awareness of Trees

The trunk, bigger than a man, stands straight,
clothed in rutted bark, majestic
in silence, invisible in sentience.

Higher up, small branches
speak strange tongues that say nothing
of living comprehension.

Yet even before winter cold
eases tight fingers, the barren twigs
put forth their daring nub.

And just as summer heat hints
vague descent, leaves are emptied,
life-giving green run to ground.

What might the tree sense,
what cognizance stirs forests
as seasons make their move?

Yet as veins appear on autumn leaves
left red, these aging hands do wonder
what might survive winter,

what knowledge might be shared,
what awareness might be gleaned,
if generosity be found in trees.

High up on some branch unseen
a small frog sits, attired in green,
waiting for the dark to sing.

Basket

Gather all the unresolvables
into a sturdy basket.
First take up the overripe angers
and greed, dripping, to line the bottom.
Next toss in bitter disappointments
and hollow regrets, washed.
Find whatever pieces of broken
promises are large enough.
Worries never help anyway
and weigh less than you might say.
Careful with hot resentments,
sharp edges of fears, thorny doubts.
Hold tight lost hopes and dreams
and secure them under
heavy responsibilities, guilts,
and weighty assumptions.
Pick all the lumps of despair,
fit them in here and there.
Scoop up sloppy mysteries
and slimy questions. They will
fill spaces between.
Cover them all with sheets of why
and blankets of unrequitedness.

Carry the basket into the deep forest.
Find there the largest of the trees
and set the basket there
on a bed of needles
among scattered cones.
Sit with it awhile and rest,
breathing the clean air.

A flash of wings here and there
high up in the crowns
may set some moments adrift.
Watch them settle with the dust of memories.
Listen for all the silence poised in wait
for just such a listener to be heard.
Feel all the loosed aches mingle
with sheets of transient rain.
Lean against an exposed root
and follow its path deep into earth.
There in hollows when freshly soaked,
awareness takes root.

Then leave the basket to empty itself
as compost for the years
and emerge at last
when the sky is ringed in gold
and ribbons of purple
line the short road home.

Parallax
(Chicago Exhibition)

There is wailing at the edges,
not knowing the future,
how dimensions shift,
expand, collapse.

In the highlighted rim
details seem more clear,
colors deepen, and yet
nothing is as it seems.

The first room is loud
with the birth of acquaintance.
Then through the halls
they come and go talking over
what they think they know,
how colors are made,
the type of brush, the life of Monet.

Walls are lined with impressions:
gardens, bright flowers,
cliffs above ocean waves,
trees reaching for the sky,
wide fields open as a palette,
soft waters reflecting
always reflecting a bridge,
or trees, or boats, sun and clouds,
or flowers, always flowers.

In the rooms they come
and go whispering wisdoms

they now know, the human context,
the angle of umbrellas,
shadows cast, always shadows.

Haystacks are the finale,
haystacks of every hue,
every season,
with shadow, without,
as if every view might be expressed
in repeating frames,
dozens of images all the same,
all different,
depending on light
always light.

The last room is silent,
quiet as the space between stars.

Who knows light but the artist,
particle and wave the same,
always the same,
duality absorbed in presence.
Who but the artist
knows the crepuscular moment,
the image that will be timeless.

There is wailing at the edges,
not knowing the past,
how dimensions shift,
expand, collapse.

At the edge where gravity bends
time and space and even light
together, reality
is just around the corner.

Barnacled Heart

The burden is in the barnacled heart
that will not let go,
that endures all the pain arthritic,
all the loss of the living,
all the ache of life alone
by turning the human twist myopic.
The burden is in the barnacled heart
that will not let go.

Like fencing grown into trees,
it seems the human paradigm
of heroes and kings,
of patterns that never had plans,
of purpose that never made sense
to live in the past tense,
this, the barnacled heart
that will not let go.

Peace appears in the unbarnacled heart
reflected like mountain peaks
on the surface of an alpine lake.
It lifts gently like morning mists
that rise in their disappearing
leaving nothing of unrepeatable pasts,
woeful or cherished, this, peace appearing
in the unbarnacled heart
that will not let go.

Like waves crashing boulders to sand,
filling every opening and gap,
it seems the living paradigm
of revolution and survival,

of adaptation in change unplanned,
of purpose living the instant aware,
this, the unbarnacled heart
reflected like mountain peaks
on the surface of an alpine lake
that will not let go.

Even on time-bound earth,
there is a precious space between,
as when between two great hills
a stream forms carrying wash
from either side away,
this heart of life that will not let go,
breathing the honest wind, that knows
high songs sung across open fields,
through high forests,
and deep ocean canyons,
this, the heart of life gleaming
in the community of smiling eyes.

Sonnet to Wind

Variant by degrees, infinite points
circling, unknown except by its absence,
who would not grasp the sound of it through pines
and fields of grain, the sound of it crashing
off coastal cliffs? And who would not keep it,
the treasure of it, gold into altars,
passed on to generations? And belief,
who would not believe in its human truth

and everlasting human permanence?
But no, it is not thus, not to be held,
not to be taught, nor even to be sought.
Ever it changes and comes unbidden,
at once unique for every living being,
at once the same in its message for all.

Ray of Light

Dust streams in the ray of sun
slanted through an open window
drifting without direction.

It might be the dust
of lost civilizations,
or a recent crumbling,
the steady shifting
of personal lives,
the slow settling of memories
to a fine, even layer.

It might be there are patterns
in the streaming
that could shape events
and change courses forever,
answers to questions
never before understood.

The slanted ray fades in darkness
to silence.

Wren song

a day like all other days
warmer than some
for February

all the troubles of the world
sit on branches around
like flocks of noisy
black birds always hungry
bickering over questions
about equality
over questions about violence
over how the earth might be pure

and more black wings come
and sharp beaks arguing
about the poor
about points of theology

morning sun the same
gleaming as most days
from every edge slanted rays
waiting for the future to come
with the swiftness of a hawk
to scatter the black flock

winter coolness
same as most February mornings
yearning for peace
yearning for a sprig of green
for a soft breath near
that might hint of life

and then miracle comes
as on some occasions
a wren hopping perch to perch
in a nearby tree
spreading a clear song
as if all the past and future
might meet
in its singular brief melody

this tiny bird
sends forth such a song
as would raise the dead
freely
to whomever would hear
leaving the air breathless

and then
a flock of sparrows
reclaims the tree
chasing the minstrel away

as if once felt
such a moment
like each and every moment
might ever be silenced

ode to the dog

we would sit, the dog and i,
in the backyard for hours,

seeing sunlight filter through trees
creating patterns in the shade,
seeing flowers in their season,
maple seeds spinning to the ground,
butterflies and ants finding their way,
squirrels running the fence,
seeing a hundred more things

and together we would listen
to wrens and sparrows in song,
cardinal proclamations,
wind through leaves ringing chimes,
neighbor children at play,
airplanes overhead, sirens on the street,
hearing a hundred more things

and together we would smell
smoke from distant hearths,
honeysuckle and moon flowers in bloom,
compost and wet earth and stone,
windy days of pollen and dust,
the faintness of rain on the way,
smelling a hundred more things

but there was always the mystery
of what her ears might hear blocks away,
what of interest was catching her eyes,
what of thousands of odors
beyond the human sense,

what intuitions she seemed to know.

sometimes we would walk the stone path
around the garden mostly with her leading
then return to sit again

little wonder we would mostly sit speechless,
little wonder, now she's gone,
i sit with an endless ache.

Wisdom

Mountain snow cannot know
of ocean waves,
but in the heated melt
finds liquid form to move
as a stream to course
rough cliffs and chasms
and traverse tangles of roots
and stones until
growing into a river irrepressible,
eases through valleys
and wide plains and finds
the shore and the greater delta
that was the answer all along.

Stream

The rock protrudes like a gravestone
marking off a great plot.

There must have been some reason
for attempts to remove it
from the middle of this stream.

Perhaps it symbolized authority,
or it was just in the way of a road.
In spite of pock-marked sides,
efforts were useless.

The noise of machines is gone
leaving the whispering stream
to wear away sharp edges.

Now the rock leans slightly
in the soft bed, ready in a moment
to be covered by the rush.

Oak Trees

Most trees by late autumn have carpeted
the forest floor with dry leaves
already into the work of compost.

But some oaks, especially the red,
though sap has run to ground,
cling to leaves like framed pictures
of children that need an update,
cling through high winds and storms,
as if the clinging were important.

Through the day those leaves
appear crisp and brown,
wrinkled with age and lost energy.

But come morning, clinging leaves
transformed by angled rays
of the early sun
shine a brilliant translucence
of red and gold,
a moment's focus

on the hidden radiance
that always awaits a change
of awareness.

Light of Day

The light that lingers
has seen it all,
disillusionment of youth,
decline of cities,
extinction of species.
The light that lingers is soft
as the edge of the horizon.

The light that opens eyes
has no edge.
Color moves in its warm smile,
hope is its message.
The light that opens eyes is fresh
as unexpected snow,
clear as lifting mists.

The light that burns
ignores inequity,
sees intent in the path,
justice in the swelter.
The light that burns
assumes renewal,
inspires visions for living.

The light that lingers
has seen it all,
passage of moments like drops
on the inevitable surface,
the increasing slant of shadows.
The light that lingers becomes,
in the darkness at the end,
the community of stars.

Mesa

Travel any road to get there
where desert descends.
When long plateaus appear,
leave the road behind
and walk past the human blight
and detritus that follow every highway.

The desert is nothing but trails
that lead there where the hot sun
leaves lessons in the sand,
lessons the sage and cacti understand.
Youth has no place there
for impatience is irrelevant;
wealth, also useless for the land
has all the wealth needed.
The hawk and rabbit and lizard
have riches beyond measure.

This is a place for the weary
and disheartened, a place
for those who have lost their way,
a place for those who mourn great loss,
or those who mourn the slow diminishing,
and those who mourn the choiceless end.

Here and there dry streams wind
their courses always sure
the rain will return.
Know their ways, and be aware,
for the sun will show
a place to sit at the edge,
just the place at a particular

shallow arroyo where the mesa,
intended mesa, best rises to the view.

Wait.
Wait the timeless wait.
The sun will come to kneel
and softer rays will touch
the edges of shoulders
and ears and feet.
Wait the timeless wait
for darkness will come
but only after.

Wait the timeless wait.
Maybe the wind will carry close
the song of a cactus wren,
the distant call of a coyote.
Maybe a breeze will whistle
through smoke bushes and creosotes.

Wait the timeless wait,
for in the soft light that smoothes
the outer edges of the mesa,
the particular mesa, there is solace,
and in the deep shadows
of the crevasses there is peace.

Ferlinghetti Aware

They sit in their rooms
writing, writing, writing
as if it mattered,
gazing up to the left,
fingers curled around pens
scratching the surface, ink sinking in,
or now again looking off to the right,
fingertips clattering letter to letter
on keys electric.

They sit in their rooms
writing, writing, writing
as if it mattered,
which, of course, it does,
just as wings of a huge flock,
fluttering like wind-tossed pages,
take off on the great migration
that changes the world;

or like the bee that drifts by
in search of a field of flowers
as provisions for a hive feast,
not knowing, perhaps, how
daisies and penstemons
and berries and fruits
rely on its busy visits,
not to mention cattle and deer
and wolves and rabbits.

And what they write
cuts deeper than swords,
proclaims freedom and equality,

when they get around to it,
usually after a polished mirror,
or mythic icon, or after a riot
is calmed or stirred up.

And what they write
describes the world,
tanks passing by windows,
aroma of bread in the morning,
gentle children at play, curious,
all the lost and lonely adrift,
joy bursting from celebrating throngs,
the strength that climbs sheer cliffs,
silent tears of sorrow in mourning,
darting fears of scattering prey,
the intimate look from sidelong eyes,
crouching tigers and soaring hawks,
dunes of heat piled dry in drifts,
the glistening at night
off rain-drenched streets.

And what they write
arises from casual gravitons
and photons in cosmic drift,
arises from amino salts intended
by plummeting asteroids,
arises from the DNA of thought
and the plasma of all that is felt.

Sometimes they sit at desks
writing, writing, writing,
or sprawled among scattered sheets,
now and again gazing out the window

at tornadic clouds moving in, gray-green,
or in the variance of time at clouds
brimming with vermilion evening.

They sit in their rooms
writing, writing, writing,
as if it mattered,
which, of course, it does,
just as the word of creation
whispered in galactic spirals
knots the fertilized dream
of salmon to the nitrogen web
that feeds bears, and trees,
and algae in the wide, wide seas.

Listen

for listening is the journey worth the seeking
the source of all that is sought.
Listen.

there it is
Listen.

beyond traffic moan
wheels on pavement
drone of passing interest
past engines over-revved
from the roar of egos
aircraft and boats howling
with the thrill of speed
past electric whine
turbines abuzz
Listen.

there beyond the noise of crowds gathered
in anger or celebration
beyond lonely sob and contented breath
beyond jubilant shout and childhood squeal
past all city noises
keep going beyond laughter of friends
beyond the mother humming to her child
low at night
Listen.

not just to music notes flying who knows
to settle far afield
not just to stories tossed about
like confetti or worse pounded

like nails to wood
not just to every human noise
Listen.

out to the countryside
keep going past fields of wheat
whispering predictions of seeds
past raucous gratch of crow
and gentle coohoo of dove
past meadowlark trill across open
and eagle cheer high in cliffs
wings flapping overhead
Listen.

keep going when wind moves leaves
and feet rustle grass
when water whispers over stones
and ocean waves crash cliffs
when elk bugle in mountain forests
and lion roar shakes the grasslands
keep going beyond whale songs
and millions of ant feet shifting sand
Listen.

past thunder shaking distance
past sheets of rain on stone
rivers booming down falls
and drops plopping into pools
past winds rushing every edge
Listen.

past every echo that cannot return
from canyon hollows
past the ether of dream

past unknowable darkness of matter
intense radiance of energy

there it is between
between stars
between minds
between words

There.

silence

listen for silence

for there may be understanding
there beyond every question aroused
by note and knock
crash and utterance
explosion and whimper
groan and sigh
curse and prayer
Listen.

language of the holy
realm of answers
silence

Listen.

Mark the Year

Mark the passing year in silence
and do not be afraid.
Loud music and furious dance
are not needed,
not bursting rockets,
nor bright flares,
nor raucous, drunken crowds.

The supposed foe so feared,
whose cold fingers grip
the edges of sanity,
is unaffected by the frenetic,
unimpressed by numbers.
It is unafraid of mindless laughter.
It relishes violent mobs.

Rather it is held at bay
outside the halo of a warm hearth.
It withdraws from a candle's
single, soft flame.
It bows before the slight breath
of the sleeping babe.

Mark the passing year in silence
and do not be afraid.
See, moments are not drops now
but flakes of snow,
an untouchable flurry
mounting into curved, high drifts.

Paradise

The story describes streets of gold
and glorious palaces,
all the pleasures lost, regained.
The story tells of innumerable rooms
and magnificent gates.
But I will be finished with walls
and unnatural light of cities
and human thoughts of grandeur.

I will dwell in holy forests
binding the roots of towering trees.
I will be long echoes
out of steep canyons
and off snow covered peaks.

I will be the exhale of howling wolves,
the intake breath of humpbacks
before they dive.
Listen, for by day I will be
the song of the finch,
by evening the cicada host,
by night the calls of frogs
one to the other.

I will boost the speed in swallow flight,
and be the curve of wind
that holds the vigilant hawk aloft.
I will be the softness of fur,
sharp spines of cacti,
smooth pebbles in streams,
gritty feel of ocean beach.

I will be the roar of water
and the calm of waveless lakes.
I will lift desert sands
and glacial snow alike.

I will be every vibration
from elephant voice to eagle cry,
ultraviolet to infrared,
radio wave to gamma ray,
rolling thunder to hummingbird wings.

I will be the luminescence
in stones and fireflies
and creatures of the deep.
I will be in every candle flame,
beams of sun between trees,
light that outlines clouds and leaves,
the flash of lightening,
and billion-year shine of stars.

If you still cant find me
I will be as close
as the next person you touch,
the next creature you hold.
And if you care to speak,
then speak, for I will be there
listening, listening to it all,
listening and laughing

with the community of life
there in the darkness
in the widening between stars.

www.ingramcontent.com/pod-product-compliance
Lightning Source LLC
Chambersburg PA
CBHW051358290426
44108CB00015B/2070